TRELLISING

HOW TO GROW CLIMBING VEGETABLES, FRUITS, FLOWERS, VINES & TREES

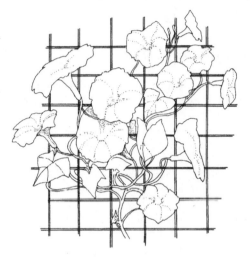

Rhonda Massingham Hart

Illustrations by Ann Poole

A Storey Publishing Book

Storey Communications, Inc.
Schoolhouse Road
Pownal, Vermont 05261

Front cover photograph by Derek Fell
Cover designed by Meredith Maker
Text designed and produced by Sherry Streeter
Line drawings by Ann Poole
Edited by Constance L. Oxley
Indexed by Gail Damerow

Printed in the United States by R. R. Donnelley
First printing, April 1992

Library of Congress Cataloging-in-Publication Data

Hart, Rhonda Massingham, 1959-
     Trellising : how to grow climbing vegetables, fruits, flowers, vines &
trees / by Rhonda Massingham Hart.
     p.   cm.
     "A Storey Publishing book."
     Includes bibliographical references and index.
     ISBN 0-88266-766-1 — ISBN 0-88266-765-3 (pbk.)
     1. Trellises.   I. Title.
SB454.H35   1992
635.9'1546—dc20   91-50606
                                            CIP

For Kailah,
The climbingest thing I know!

CONTENTS

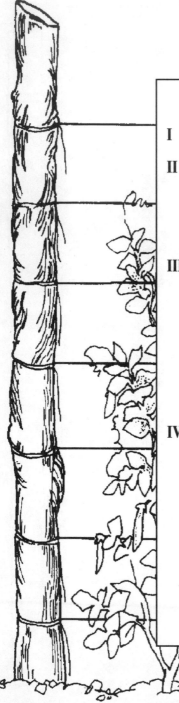

INTRODUCTION

Y̲ou have seen them. Those gorgeous, elaborate examples of trellised plants beckon, even if only from the pages of the latest garden magazine. Images of ethereal, billowing green and pink clouds of climbing roses, obediently outstretched arms and fingers of espaliered fruit trees, or cascading waves of wisteria reach from their pages to flirt with our imaginations and tug at our envious hearts. Such visions of the gardener's devotion are surely beyond us, the Keepers of the Home Plot, so pressed for time, space, and available resources. Or are they?

True, creating these living works of art takes time and dedication, both things today's backyard gardener may find in short supply. But the techniques that are used in achieving these glorious results can be put to good use even by the most hurried of home growers. The results may be less dramatic with trellised beans or cucumbers, but that depends entirely on one's perspective. Whether you trellis plants for fine art or fine harvests, one of the most appreciable results will be one less harried, less tired, more satisfied gardener!

The principles of trellising garden crops are few and simple. Climbing stems or vines are trained onto upright supports either by means of their own climbing growth habits or by being tied in place. A support, or trellis, generally consists of standards, or a frame, and plant supports. The trellis may be a permanent structure or a seasonal garden fixture.

While training perennial vines to a trellis is a gradual process, single season crops and flowers, such as tomatoes, squash, peas, or nasturtiums yield more immediate results. Whether you seek a single season of fruit or years of blooming, scented satisfaction, there is a vine for you!

Anyone who has ever staked a tomato plant has trained a vine crop to a trellis. Whether or not that same gardener followed through with tying, pinching off suckers, plucking late blossoms, feeding, watering, and frost protection is a different matter. The best results require attention to all of these things.

Trellising does more than just tidy up the garden or free up space. Restricting the random sprawl of ground-robbing vines by training them up a framework provides both the plants and the gardener with many benefits. More light and increased air movement improve plant growth and health. Less ground space used makes for less work, more efficient watering, and easier pest control. The trellis can serve as a frame for other coverings or as a shaded respite for a weary gardener. The bottom line, however, is bigger, better, and easier harvests.

This book will show you the best materials to use and how to use them. Basic designs and plans for different types of trellises and which plants are most suited to them are also covered. A gallery of some of the best candidates for trellising follows under headings for each specific crop or ornamental plant. All of this follows the most straightforward explanation of why you should be trellising these crops right now and for all your growing seasons to come. You will thoroughly enjoy this upward trend and wonder what took you so long to Grow Up!

CLIMBING ADVANTAGES

Don't have room for sprawling pumpkin vines? Settling for bush beans instead of the variety of colors, textures, and tastes that are offered by pole beans? Don't savor the idea of tangled masses of space-hogging vines of cucumbers, melons, or rambling squash? Free yourself to grow whatever your heart desires. No matter how little square footage you have in your garden, chances are that you have been totally overlooking most of your available growing area—that often neglected vertical space.

MAKE THE MOST OF LESS SPACE

Every square foot of garden space comes with the bonus of up to 6 cubic feet of usable growing space, assuming you can reach 6 feet high. The actual ground space taken up by any one vine may be reduced to just 1 or 2 square inches. This leaves the remainder of the area that would otherwise be occupied by straggling vines to be put to other uses, such as planting more crops!

Of course, extra demands on the same plot of earth will require a little more attention to the health of the soil. Increased nutritional demands of these extra plants mean more of a drain on the soil's available nutrients. Organic practices, such as composting, growing and tilling under green manure crops, top dressing with seasoned animal manures, or treating growing plants to an occasional cup of fish emulsion, will not only replace the extra nutrients used, but also will increase the content of organic matter in the soil and improve its texture and drainage. Plants that are grown in soil rich in organic matter are also usually less vulnerable to soilborne pests.

CULTIVATE LESS GROUND—
LESS WEEDING, UPKEEP & TIME

Even though you may already be utilizing every conceivable square inch of your garden space to produce all those ground greedy crops, there is another significant benefit to growing those same plants on trellises. If space is not a concern, perhaps the difference is in gardener work load.

Using less ground space means maintaining less ground space. There is less area to produce competitive plant life, which directly translates into less weeding. There is also less area to mulch, fence, and generally wear out the gardener. Using less garden space also means spending less time doing all those gardening chores. It also means freeing up some of your valuable real estate for other things, like a hammock!

CREATE A SHADY SPACE

Perhaps just the spot for the gardener to rest his or her weary bones is in the shade of a grape arbor or trellised blackberries or cherry tomatoes. Consider installing a well-deserved garden bench. Of course, how you utilize your tailor-made shade is up to you. Many plants appreciate a shaded spot in the plot. You may decide to add a patch of salad greens, spinach, or a cole crop. You could provide a birdbath or a small garden pond to pamper some of your garden guests.

PROVIDE A FRAMEWORK FOR PLANT COVERINGS

Besides providing the structural support for climbing vines, a trellis can provide a framework for various plant coverings. Draping clear plastic over tomato cages, for example, transforms them into individual cloches, or minigreenhouses. The sun's rays pass through the covering and heat the air around tender transplants. The warmer, inside air temperature allows the gardener to transplant much earlier by using this season extender. As fall temperatures cool, plants can again be covered to extend that end of the season.

The trellis frame also can be used as a windbreak. Often young transplants are battered mercilessly by untimely spring gales. Draping a tarp, blanket, or any available covering over the trellis frame will shield young plants from the occasional spring wind storm.

One of the most effective cover-ups for your trellis frame is an insect-proof garden fabric. Many types are sold through garden supply stores and catalogues. All are lightweight, allow for maximum penetration of sunlight and water, and bar bugs, birds, and small varmints from trespassing. The cover-ups, which are made of spun bonded polypropelene, will also pull double duty as season extenders by keeping the air temperature underneath several degrees higher than the outside air.

Such coverings allow tender seedlings or transplants to get off to a strong, growing start without the danger of succumbing to frosts or pests. Care must be taken, however, to remove the covers to allow for pollination and vine growth and to prevent warming temperatures from precooking your produce under those heat-retaining layers.

WATER MORE EFFICIENTLY

One of the most common methods of watering home gardens is also one of the most wasteful. Overhead sprinklers can be especially inefficient on the broad leaves of many of the most popular plants for trellising, such as squash or cucumbers. The wide leaves divert the spray away from the root area of the plants and send it splashing off onto yet more leaves. In order to thoroughly water your pumpkin patch this way, many hundreds of gallons of water will be lost to those detour-producing leaves. Evaporation as the water sails from the sprinkler head toward thirsty plants will also claim a fair amount of moisture.

Vines that are trained politely up a trellis are much easier to water without waste. The soil line near the stem of the plant is exposed so that water can penetrate to the roots. Any one of several, efficient methods can be used. Drip irrigation lines can be placed around the base of trained vines. One can partially bury a bucket, a plastic milk jug, a large-sized coffee can, or other suitable container near the vines at transplant time. Drill or punch small holes in the bottom of the container to allow for slow, constant drainage; fill periodically with water to provide steady moisture for growing vines.

INCREASE LIGHT & AIR

Not only does training your vines upward allow for more sunlight to reach those energy-gathering leaves, but also it allows for freer movement of the air surrounding the leaves. Vines growing along the ground create a moist, still microenvironment underneath their canopy of overlapping leaves. This is a perfect environment for many disease organisms and damaging fungi. Many of these diseases are spread by wind, splashing water, pest vectors, or physical contact as the gardener works around the plants. Cool, wet conditions often rapidly encourage the spread of disease.

Elevating the foliage and training it along a trellis can effectively eliminate a prime source of contamination—ground contact. Also, it can significantly reduce a major cause of plant-to-plant transmission—moist, overlapping growth. Air circulates more freely among the raised vines and leaves and keeps their surfaces drier, which helps to keep diseases from starting or spreading.

MONITOR & MANAGE PESTS MORE EASILY

Dozens of pests abound to terrorize our carefully tended crops. Many brazenly take advantage of the plant's growth habit and hide among the spreading foliage. Pests thrive in the moist, shaded microclimate that those ground-hugging plants provide. Various borers damage plants by first chewing a hole in the vine near where the stem meets the ground. Plants that ramble aimlessly about the garden offer nearly unlimited access because a great deal of the surface area of the vines is in contact with the soil. Pulling these errant stems off the ground and guiding them over vertical supports drastically reduces potential entry points to *one*, which is much easier to watch over than dozens or hundreds of leaf obscured possibilities.

Skybound vines are visually easier to inspect at a glance than their grounded, unkempt cousins. Bugs are easier to spot on orderly trained vines than on overlapping tangles of vegetation. Raising the vines off the ground makes the job physically easier, too. Rather than hunching and bending and continually shoving wayward growth from your path, your inspection of a neatly trained, trellised vine often requires little more than a quick nod of your head and a flick of a few leaves. With a major share of the plant's growth at or near eye level, the task is greatly reduced.

Trellised plants are not only easier to check for pests, but also are more efficiently treated. Any sprays or dusts that you may need to apply can be administered to a smaller area with a greater amount of the plant's surface area exposed. This reduces the amounts of insecticides used. Application of insecticides is also simplified by not having to fight sprawling, ankle-grabbing vegetation. You eliminate the risk of accidentally stepping on and crushing vines or fruit that might otherwise get underfoot.

GAIN HIGHER YIELDS

Two separate strategies are at work here. First, although plant breeders are always striving for improvement in disease resistance, taste, and yields of new, compact varieties of everything from bush beans to patio tomatoes, often the old-time varieties consistently outperform the newcomers. The bush or compact varieties are generally the great-great-grandchildren of vining ancestors. The vining varieties of everything from peas and beans to tomatoes and squash are most often genetically superior and produce more, better tasting fruit over a longer period of time than competing, compact cousins.

Second, even without overwhelming evidence from repeated research, it is not difficult to understand why, given two identical plants, one grown using conventional methods and the other trained up a trellis, the trellised plant will surpass the other. What a privileged life it leads! The trellised plant receives a steady water supply and is kept pest free. It may also be disease free due to the increased aeration around its leaves. It is kept free from undue nutrient and light competition because it is much easier to weed. Perhaps it will be afforded a snugly crop cover to keep it cozy, even though it was planted in the garden weeks before its twin. Under its shade, the gardener may install a lovely garden bench on which he or she may pause to admire and talk to the lucky vine. With all of these advantages, how could it not produce higher yields!

PRODUCE THE EARLIEST, CLEANEST & LONGEST LASTING HARVESTS

Which would you rather do: stoop to twist an overgrown squash from its prickly vine, that until this moment had gone totally unnoticed in its leafy, hiding place, only to find the bottom rotted from resting in the damp earth, or reach out and pluck yet another perfect specimen as it dangles freely away from the vine, inches from your nose?

As vines are trained up their trellises, the fruit, being heavier than other parts of the vine, hangs away from the structure. Trellises can be designed for anything from overhead grape arbors to A framelike, cucumber supports. Those that provide either a horizontal or sloped, growing area will allow the fruit to hang freely down and away from the trellis.

MATERIALS

Choosing the building materials for your garden trellises depends on: how much you can spend on aesthetics; if you are building a temporary (single season) structure or a permanent addition to the garden; what type of plants you want to support.

Many gardeners tend to be "creatively frugal" by recycling anything from used baling twine to the plastic rings that hold beverage cans together. Turning trash into trellises may not be as visually appealing as a custom-made, redwood, grape arbor, but both forms can serve their primary purpose equally well. Utilize whatever building materials are available. Creative designing and lush, healthy foliage will soon obscure any less-than-attractive components.

Most trellises are composed of two basic parts in a wide range of variations. The frame is usually constructed of stiff, sturdy, weight-bearing material, such as lumber, metal, or heavy bamboo. The frame defines the form of the structure as well as holding up the plant support, which may be made from light, flexible material, such as twine, netting, wire, or the same material as the frame.

FRAMEWORK

Wood is by far the most common material that is used in building trellis frames. It is sturdy and good looking and some types will last a lifetime. It is not cheap, especially if you are careful to select the best wood, but the more expensive kinds of wood will repay you with years of service.

The best woods to use in the garden are cedar, redwood, black locust, cypress, spruce, osage orange, and oak—any of these may last for decades. All are more weather resistant than cheaper pine or fir, which will rot in a few years if left untreated. When pressure treated, pine and fir will last longer, but may be saturated with chemicals that you may not want to introduce into your garden. Look for copper naphthenate (Cuprinol) when selecting treated wood; it releases no harmful chemicals. You may save money by substituting scrap lumber for new, but take care in using any old wood that has been painted. Old paint may be lead based—toxic to both people and plants.

To extend the life of wooden trellises, design them to knock down and store away when not in use, and keep them out of winter weather. Also, when using wooden posts for standards, try substituting round, pointed fence posts for the elite woods. Set them in the ground pointed side up to prevent water from collecting in any dents or fissures in the top and allowing rot to set in. No matter what type of wood that you choose for your trellis, look for posts cut from the center of the tree—the heartwood. Untreated heartwood posts last twice as long as untreated wood cut from the outside edges—the sapwood.

Galvanized steel fence posts come in various lengths from 4 to 8 feet long and are readily available in farm stores. Perhaps not as good looking as wooden posts, they are easy to put in, easy to take out, last forever and, most importantly, do the job.

Metal pipe, either salvaged or purchased new, is also good framing material. Galvanized pipe will outlast nongalvanized pipe, except in seaside areas. The pipe can be driven into the soil and when necessary, easily removed. Fittings, such as T's, Y's, and elbows, give the trellis designer many options. Short pieces can be connected, corners, arms, or extensions can be added, and entire sections can be fitted together or altered. A little elbow grease and a hacksaw are all that is needed to shorten any long pieces. Some designs that use pipe incorporate an underground portion that is drilled with drainage holes to irrigate the plants at root level (see page 11).

PVC pipe may win even more votes as a suitable, framing material counterpart. PVC (polyvinyl chloride) comes in many sizes and shapes, rigid and thick-walled, or thin and flexible varieties. Like metal pipe, fittings make it easy to plan a multitude of useful, garden designs from full-scale arbors to individual plant cages. Whether you like the looks of PVC is your decision, but it is very durable and reasonably priced.

Bamboo is lightweight and weathers as well or better than scrap lumber. It tends to split, though, if you try to bend it, especially if it is cold.

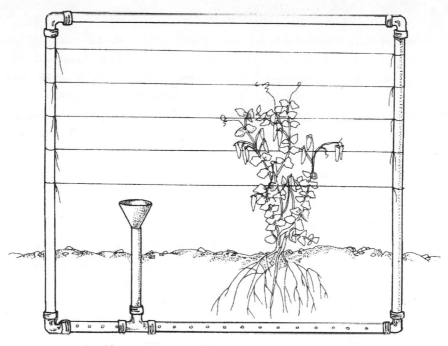

A self-supporting, self-watering, metal pipe trellis

Compared to most other materials, it is very inexpensive. Bamboo can be grown at home to provide you with lots of free building material. Just as attractive as wood, it can be used in many designs as both framing and support material.

A range of ready-made trellising materials are currently on the market. Telescoping fiberglass stakes can stretch from 2 ½ to 5 feet long. Circular, metal tomato cages fit over small plants and support them as the plants grow through the rings. Tuteurs are epoxy coated steel forms, 70 inches tall, and are available in a four-legged tower or a single pole with an umbrellalike top (both are expensive). Wire mesh products include Vertical Veggies, which are heavy gauge, 6-inch black wire mesh panels that are sold in sets of four. Each panel is 18 inches wide by 36 inches high and comes with nylon connectors that can be linked into square cages or into tall, vertical panels. Another wire mesh product is Trellex, which are plastic coated panels from 1 to 4 feet wide and 6 feet long. Other trellising materials, including ready-made A frames with netting and complete arch and arbor kits, are available by mail order or through local, nursery outlets. See Appendix II for suppliers of these and other useful items.

SUPPORTS

The type of plant support that is used in your design, like the material used for framing, depends greatly on the type of plant that it must support. Most garden crops can be trained up twine, netting wire, or wire mesh. More expensive, wooden lattice is often used for permanent, landscaping trellises that are destined for the swarming vines of clematis, wisteria, climbing rose, or grapes. I advise you to avoid any thin, lightweight, or flimsy string, such as kite string, because the weight of growing vines will break it. Or the reverse problem occurs when fine, taut string cuts through tender, growing vines, cuts off the plant's circulation, and kills the vine.

Twine, technically defined as "heavy string," is a garden trellis institution. Heavy-duty jute is a natural, compostable fiber and is always available and fairly cheap. Nylon seine twine, cotton cable cord, vinyl coated, clothesline wire are all reusable possibilities. Miles of baling twine are cast out everyday by livestock owners who would probably be very happy to have you remove it for them. (You may pick up some free fertilizer in the bargain!) Check out stables, race tracks, dairies, hobby farms, petting zoos, or anyone who may feed their animals hay. Alfalfa is often put up in heavier bales and held with wire rather than twine; this wire is flexible, lightweight, and strong enough to weave into a trellis design.

If you have lots of old rope lying around, such as nylon, plastic, jute, or braided or plaited anything, it will do nicely for plant supports. Natural fibers, however, tend to swell and shrink as they get wet then dry and are susceptible to rot. Ready-made netting for garden trellises is sold through mail-order catalogues and garden supply stores (see Appendix II). It is woven of strong, weatherproof nylon with large 6- to 7-inch square openings to allow for easy pruning, tying, inspecting, and harvesting. Available in different widths and lengths, it is moderately priced and will last many seasons.

Wire can be substituted for twine or netting and for some plants is the first choice. Ten-gauge copper or galvanized wire, $3/_{16}$-inch vinyl coated, tiller cable, guy wire, baler wire, or salvaged electrical or telephone wire can be strung along your frames.

Wire mesh fencing is also great for incorporating into a trellis. Galvanized, woven wire mesh (also called sheep or hog wire) will perform admirably, has a rustic look, will last for years, and is more rust resistant and more expensive than nongalvanized wire mesh, such as concrete reinforcing wire. Oceanside gardeners, however, need not waste their money on galvanized wire mesh because it tends to deteriorate more quickly in damp, salty air.

One important thing to remember when using either galvanized or nongalvanized wire or fencing is to match the fencing to the fasteners. Always use galvanized nails or staples with galvanized wire and nongalvanized fasteners with nongalvanized fencing to prevent corrosion at contact points.

It is very important to always choose a wire with a large enough mesh (4- to 6-inch openings) to comfortably fit your hand through. Smaller mesh wire presents two equally frustrating problems. First, a tighter mesh may not allow the fruits of your labor to be easily tended or picked. No amount of swearing will pull a 4-inch-wide squash through a 2-inch-square hole! Second, pulling dead vines out of small wire mesh is a chore that no gardener needs added to his or her list of fall cleanup duties.

One drawback to wire or wire mesh is that it is not always suitable for quick growing, *tender*, annual vines. The wire gets very hot under the summer sun and can burn the sensitive vines and foliage. Try to use another type of support for tender plants.

Wood lathing or poles can be used for plant supports in designs from arbors and arches to tepee-style trellises. Thinned saplings also make excellent rustic poles and, if peeled and cured in the sun, will last for several seasons.

Bamboo also can be used as plant supports and gives a rustic/exotic look and a durable future to any trellis.

TIES, CLIPS & SLINGS

Some plants climb by means of spiraling tendrils or leafstalks, some by stems that weave in and out of available supports or that wrap around them, and still others have devised aerial, rootlike holdfasts or tiny, adhesive pads that cling to their supporting surface. Any of these, at some point, may need a little assist in staying aloft.

A variety of ties, clips, slings, and other accessories can be used in training upwardly mobile vines. For garden crops, usually all that is needed is to gently guide the stems to the support and watch them climb. Some, however, need to be tied in place as they grow. Jute cord, plastic ties, paper covered, wire twist ties, vinyl covered wire or twine, and strips of cloth or

Types
of
Climbers

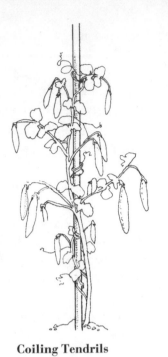

Coiling Tendrils

Twining Leafstalks

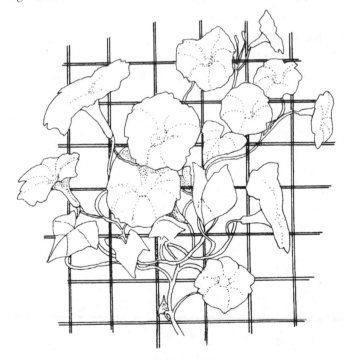

Weaving Stems

Twining Stems

Rootlike Holdfasts

Adhesive Discs

discarded nylons can be put to good use.

Also of prime importance is the way in which the tie is used. Never tie vines snugly to their supports because this will constrict the vascular system of the plant and cut off the flow of nutrients to any part of the plant that follows the knot. Slip knots are not recommended either because they may accidentally tighten with the same results. Learn to tie a proper square knot. Then loop the tie first around the support and then around the plant stem.

Seed catalogues and garden supply stores offer plastic twist ties and clips especially made for securing delicate plant stems to trellises, stakes, fencing, or twine (see Appendix II). The twist ties come in spools that allow you to cut off any desired length, and the pinch-on clips are packaged in quantities of six to twenty-five or more, which makes either product economical.

The fruit of some vines may require additional support as it grows. Some squash and pumpkins may pull on the trellised vines and cause them to sag or break. Why risk the unnecessary splattering of a prize melon when a little prevention will stop the unthinkable. Old panty hose, sheets, pillow-cases, bird netting, macramé, or any other handy fabric can be fashioned into a life-saving sling. Cut the material to the appropriate size for your fruit, which is judged by its predicted size and weight at maturity. Tie one end securely to the plant support and loosely fit the fabric under the fruit; center it in the sling as much as possible. Tie the other end of the sling to the plant support so that the fruit rests loosely and comfortably in its little hammock (see illustration on page 17).

Other hardware that you may need in building your trellis or managing your vines can include nails and staples, turnbuckles to keep weight-bearing wires taut, eyebolts and wire rope clips to hold wires or twine, hinges and floor flanges, or other fastening devices to secure wires in place.

CONTAINERS

It is true that many gardeners turn to trellising crops because they are short on space and then realize the other genuine bonuses that trellising provides. But if you are really squeezed for ground space, perhaps to where you feel that you cannot even consider vine crops or fruit trees, consider container gardening.

Almost anything that can be trellised can be reared in some type of

Melon Sling

planter box. Many plans for planters incorporate the trellis right into the design. Containers, such as large clay or fiber pots, redwood boxes, half wine barrels, etc., can be purchased, and the trellis can be attached or driven into the ground or fastened to a nearby wall. Be sure that the container has never contained any type of toxic substance. Drill holes in the bottom for adequate drainage and place in a sunny spot.

Container growing eliminates many of the standard concerns of site and soil and has a dwarfing effect on large plants and fruit trees. It also presents some unique challenges. You cannot simply shovel in dirt from the garden and expect to reap a bumper crop. Even the best garden soil tends to clump and compact in the confines of a container. Nevertheless, when filled with a good, loose potting soil, either purchased or prepared by thoroughly amending your best garden loam with organic matter, peat, sand, or perlite to promote good aeration and drainage, containers have a lot in their favor. Drainage is excellent. The roots may dry out quickly, however, if not watched carefully. In moisture-wicking clay or fiber pots, the soil warms much more quickly than at ground level. Of course, the most obvious advantage is the limited space requirements. Many plants from patio tomatoes to miniature fruit trees can be grown successfully in only a few feet of ground space.

When selecting plants for containers, remember that many require cross-pollination, which means that they will not set fruit unless pollinated by another plant, often of a different variety. Apple, pear, apricot, and sweet cherry trees and some types of cucumbers are good examples. The plants should either be grown with pollinators nearby or have branches of pollinating varieties grafted on. For example, up to five similar varieties can be grown on one little fruit tree. Now that is saving space!

TRELLIS DESIGNS

The way that you design your trellises depends on several things. You must consider the type of plant that will be trained to the trellis, the materials that you have to work with, and the style of the trellis. Nature and finances may rule the first two considerations, but style is limited only by your imagination and the laws of physics.

Picture an arch framed, garden gate that is overflowing with bright, fragrant climbing roses. What could be lovelier? To the avid recycler, bean towers that are built from old bicycle wheels or a pea trellis that is fashioned from a discarded mattress frame may be just as beautiful a sight. In the garden, function is at least as important as form. To a gardener, any healthy vine that is winding up any type of trellis is a pretty sight.

STAKES

The simplest of all plant supports are stakes or poles. They are driven into the soil near the base of the plant, and the vines instinctively latch onto them. Tomato stakes and bean poles are classic examples. Tie the plant to the stake to support the vine as it grows to the full length of the stake; then prune the excess growth at the top.

Garden centers usually offer a range of wooden, bamboo, or manufactured stakes that are suitable for training tomatoes, beans, nasturtiums, sweet peas, and other annual vines. Scrap lumber in 1x2 or 2x2 sizes, pieces of metal or PVC pipe, or other thin, rigid material sometimes can be commandeered for service.

TEPEES

There is a primitive beauty in growing greenery that swirls its way up the legs of a tepee support. The ancient design conjures up images of gardeners of long ago. The form lends itself to many plants, from beans, peas, or tomatoes to honeysuckle, trumpet vines, or climbing roses to heavily fruited crops, such as melons and squash. Many vines may be supported on sapling poles or bamboo, but those that bear heavy fruit demand a sturdier structure.

Building a tepee support is quick, easy, and inexpensive. You will need 3 to 6 poles—thin ones for flowers, peas, or beans and stouter ones for squash, melons, or heavy sweet potato vines. Cut the poles 10 to 12 feet long to have at least 1 or 2 feet to sink into the ground to solidly anchor the finished tepee. Use twine, raffia, or strips of rawhide or cloth to lash the poles together near the top. Pull the poles into a tight bundle, wrap the twine around the bundle a few times, and tie it snugly. Prop the bundle of poles over the planting area, and position the bottom ends so that each pole will support 1 or 2 vines.

If you are using large poles, 2 to 3 inches across, they are heavy enough to be freestanding. There is usually no need to drive them into the soil. Their extra weight makes it nearly impossible to erect the tepee all at once; instead, tie the poles together in twos. You will need a helper to hold up the first set of two while you straddle it with the second set, arrange the legs, then wrap the tops together. A four-legged tepee (two sets of two poles) works wonderfully for squash, melons, and sweet potatoes.

Additional support for heavy vines can be worked into a tepee design by wrapping heavy twine or rope around one leg of the structure near the bottom and by continuing up and around toward the top (see page 21).

Another variation on the tepee method is a running tepee. Running tepees are great for long, wide rows of crops. To build, start with either a pole tepee at either end of the row or a post (a height of 6 feet will accommodate most crops). Tie a long, thin pole to the top of the end tepees or posts so that it connects the two, or string a heavy wire or rope between the tops of the posts and tighten. The last step is to lean the poles (saplings, scrap 1x2s, or bamboo are perfect) along the length of the connecting pole in pairs and tie each pair together at the top (see page 21).

Seed directly or transplant along the length of each row that is created by the feet of the tepee poles.

FENCES

Fences are among the easiest, most versatile, and most used trellises that

Tepee-style Trellis

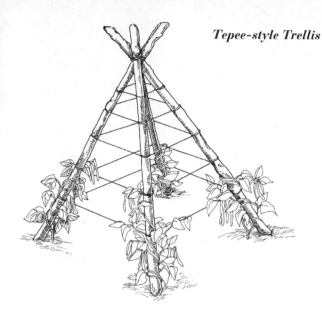

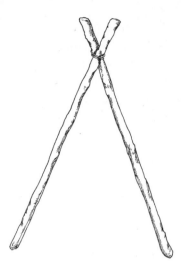

**Sturdy pole tepee trellis
with twine support added**

Two poles lashed together

Running Tepee

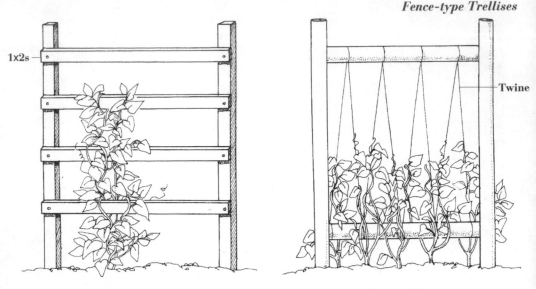

1x2s

Twine

Wooden Posts

Plastic Pipe

are found in gardens everywhere. Drive a post at each end of a row, and place other posts in between where needed. String with twine, wire, netting, or wire mesh, and you have a fence-type trellis. The standards, or end posts, can be anything from wood or metal fence posts to pipe or, in a pinch, existing trees. Tie, wire, staple, or nail a plant support to the standards so that it is taut enough to hold the vines without sagging.

Many trellises, from stake and netting, dwarf pea fences to freestanding post and wire espalier trellises, follow this very basic design. Some need bracing at the end posts or additional posts in between. Fences over 20 feet long should have installed an extra post every 10 to 12 feet.

CLOTHESLINE TRELLIS

By attaching crossarms to the end posts and running wires between them, the simple fence trellis is converted into a clothesline trellis that can support two or four lines instead of just one. This type of trellis allows you to plant double rows and is useful for many annual crops and berry brambles. Since the posts in clothesline trellises (double fences) must bear twice the weight of those in a simple fence, it is a good idea to brace them at each end.

of Various Materials

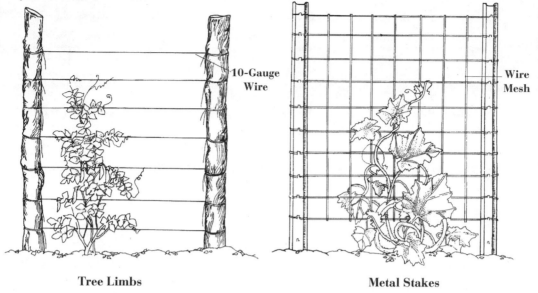

10-Gauge
Wire

Wire
Mesh

Tree Limbs

Metal Stakes

Clothesline Trellis

CAGES

Another simple and efficient method of containing errant sprawlers is with a cage. Cages can be nailed together from scrap 1x2 lumber or made with wire mesh. Choose a wire mesh that is sturdy enough to retain its shape under the weight of vines and fruit. Bend the mesh into an arch shape, and arrange it over transplants, such as tomatoes or cucumbers.

Round or square cages, 2 to 3 feet in diameter and 3 to 4 feet high, will both contain and support a variety of vines. To figure the total length of mesh to cut for a cylindrical cage, use the formula: $C = 2\pi r$. That is, the circumference (distance around) of the cylinder is 2 times π (3.14) times the radius (half the total diameter of the circle). More simply, multiply the diameter of the cylinder that you want to make by 6.28. For instance, for a 3-foot-wide cage, you would need 3 × 6.28 or 18.84 feet of wire and for a 4-foot-wide cage, 4 × 6.28 or 25.12 feet of wire. Connect snaps to the ends of the mesh and snap the cylinders together, or add a few inches to the final measurement and bend the wire back over the opposite end of the mesh to hold it in place. Drive a stake into the ground through the wire mesh to anchor the support against the wind (see page 25).

Cage Variations

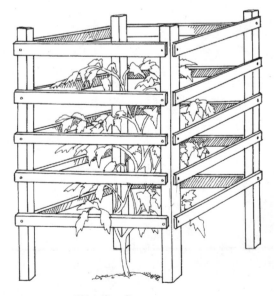

Wooden Square

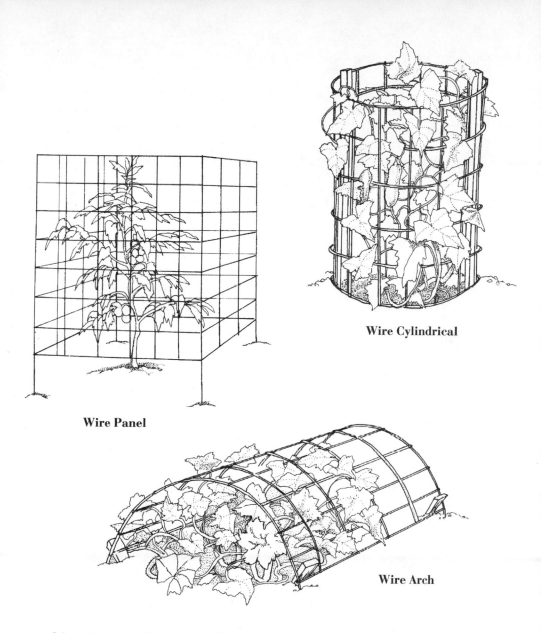

Wire Cylindrical

Wire Panel

Wire Arch

   More intricate designs can be constructed by using lighter weight wire and wooden frames or by cutting the wire mesh into individual panels and wiring them together into freestanding square cages. The advantage to panel-type cages is that they can be taken apart for storage. For square- or panel-type cages, multiply the width of the cage by 4, and cut the wire accordingly. Again, you may wish to add a few inches to overlap and connect the ends.

A FRAMES

Here is another extremely useful, versatile, and easily constructed garden trellis. By incorporating either hinges or pivot nails into the top of an A frame trellis, it can be folded together. This makes the trellis a snap to move and store and allows the gardener to rotate climbing garden vines.

Another advantage to the A frame design is that both sides of the trellis are used and the shaded corridor that is created between the sides is a perfect spot to plant some greens, which makes the row more productive.

Depending on the type of materials that are used, this is a wonderful, all-purpose trellis. It can be made sturdy enough to support even heavy crops, such as gourds or pumpkins. By changing its position in the garden every year, the same structure can be used to support cucumbers one year, squash the next, then tomatoes, and later beans or peas. It can pull double duty as the framework for shade cloth and bug-proof or bird-proof crop covers, or it can be made into an instant greenhouse by tacking clear, plastic sheeting to the frame. If versatility were not blessing enough from this useful design, consider that the pattern can be built of scraps, which adds economy to the list of advantages.

Construct the A frame of lightweight lumber—1x2s or 2x4s. Wire mesh fencing, garden netting, or vertically or horizontally strung wire or twine will all serve well as the plant support. While you may design an

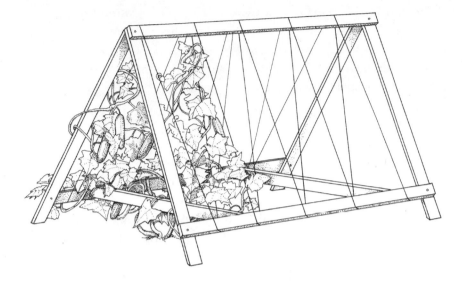

A frame in any dimensions to suit your site, bear in mind that if it is to be portable, it must be of manageable size. Better to build and move four 6-foot components than one 24-foot monster.

A simplified version of an A frame is popular for cucumbers and squash. Cut stiff, self-supporting wire in 6 to 8 foot lengths, and using a straightedge, such as a board or pipe, bend the panels in the middle to form a V. Flip the panels over, and place several V bends along the row so that the ends are a few inches apart. This creates an uninterrupted zigzag trellis. Set the transplants in the spaces between the individual cages, and train the vines up the sides of the cage on either side.

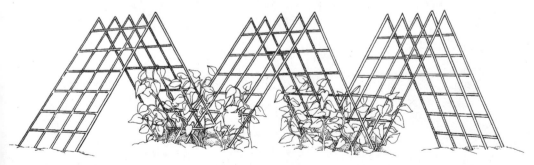

Zigzag Trellis

ARCHES & ARBORS

Whether you envision lush grapes, exotic wisteria, or romantic old country roses, most of us, when we dally on such thoughts, picture them clamoring over some classic, old arbor. Garden books and magazines are fairly bursting with patterns of beautiful, permanent, landscape trellises. Often these indulgent structures serve as the focal point of the garden and set either a formal, informal, or rustic tone.

Choosing deciduous plants to climb the trellises will create shade in the summer, while still allowing the sun to shine through in the winter. Permanent vines can dominate the trellis, or annual vines can be trained or worked in among longtime residents. So although the structure is permanent, it can still be varied and versatile.

Architectural designs range from the rustic to prim Victorian or sleek contemporary. You might lash peeled, wooden branches together for a rustic look or create swooping scrolls and archways for a formal approach. Attach an arched trellis to a bare wall to convert it instantly into an elegant backdrop. Consider, however, attaching this elegant trellis with hinges or pivot bolts so that it can swing down if you ever need to get to that wall.

The horizontal beams of an arbor provide not only a support for vines,

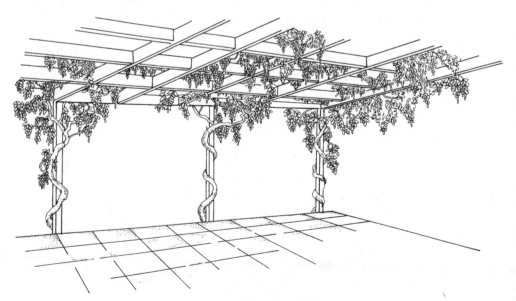

Arbor

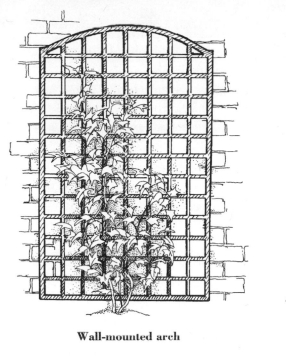

Wall-mounted arch

Arch

but also a secluded, shady spot for the gardener. Doorways, paths, patios, gazebos, or any other special, outdoor area can be transformed with a vine covered archway. Consider including a planter box in your designs, and enjoy the added benefits of raised beds. Create a private corner with an arch or arbor, or use it as camouflage for whatever you may wish to hide. Living screens are also an excellent means of providing a windbreak or, to the often overwhelmed city dweller, a much needed noise and/or pollution barrier.

Despite the nearly limitless possibilities for arbor design and construction, the gardener must always weigh the basic considerations of expense and the intended climbers. Posts should be driven or dug 24 to 30 inches deep or set in at least 18 inches of concrete. Vertical supports should be well anchored with galvanized nails or screws to the horizontal beams that define the frame of the trellis. Overhead, horizontal supports must be strong enough to bear the weight of the vines; a double layer of crisscross lattice is sturdy and attractive.

Ease of maintenance should also be considered not only for pruning, harvesting, or spraying the plants, but also for upkeep on the trellis and any existing background structures. Brackets, bolts, hinges, and other hardware add somewhat to the initial investment, but will go a long way toward making routine gardening chores easier by making the trellis movable.

ESPALIER FRAMES

Although conventionally accepted practice throughout Europe, the gardener's art of espalier is often regarded as somewhat ostentatious in the United States, but this is changing. Although most gardeners are drawn to the challenge or beauty of espalier, what hooks them is the undeniable practicality of this fine, garden art.

Designing the pattern into which trees are to be trained depends more on the tree than on the type of trellis. Most espaliered trees are trained on a heavy wire, fencelike frame. The copper wire (12 to 14 gauge is the most highly recommended) can be strung between sturdy wood or metal posts or through eyebolts or flanges that are attached directly to an existing wall or fence. Wooden lattice works fine and is more attractive in the early stages, but will soon be obliterated by foliage, blossoms, and fruit.

Trees may be trained in the open, but are frequently seen espaliered against a wall. A wall often helps by providing a windbreak and by reflecting light and heat back toward the tree. Ideally, espalier frames should be erected at least 6 inches from an existing structure to allow for adequate ventilation, growth, and room for the gardener to work. Stone, brick, stucco, aluminum siding, or untreated wooden walls are the best candidates. Once an espaliered tree is established, any painting or maintenance to the walls is next to impossible.

A standard fence-type frame (see illustration on page 23), with 8-foot posts sunk about 2 feet deep, 8 to 10 feet apart and strung with 1 to 6 strands of wire on eyebolts at 15- to 24-inch intervals, can serve as a basic espalier trellis for many types of trees. Turnbuckles attached to one end of each wire will assure constant tension and therefore an absolutely straight line, which is imperative for formal patterns. By gradually tying and repositioning the growing tips of branches, or cordons, and pruning them according to the envisioned result, you can create an endless variety of beautiful, intriguing, and vastly productive, tree shapes.

CLINGING VINES

A surprising variety of crops are suitable for trellising. You probably would not be surprised that beans and peas are perfectly suited to this method of growing. You also might know that bramble berries can be trained to a trellis. Perhaps the notion of trellising ground greedy cucumbers or squash has occurred to you. But would you believe there is a variety of spinach that climbs? Would you expect to see heavy melons or pumpkins suspended in midair? What about sweet potatoes? (No, the spuds do not rise above their lowly position, but the rowdy vines will enthusiastically swarm a trellis.) And if you are really ready for something a little different, imagine hardy kiwi vines trailing along that trellis.

Now that we know just how much better the plants will do on a trellis than on the ground, and we have considered the various building materials and methods, it is time to select some plants and get growing!

BASELLA MALABAR RED STEM

For something truly unique and tasty, try basella malabar red stem summer spinach. Native to parts of Africa and Southeast Asia, this unusual vegetable is featured in the display gardens at the world famous, Epcot Center at Walt Disney World in Florida. It makes a wonderful, summer spinach substitute; it flourishes in the hot weather that makes regular spinach wilt. The dark green, fleshy leaves and bright red stems have a mild flavor and are delicious.

This handsome plant may well become the centerpiece of your garden since it is as distinctively attractive as it is productive. The lush green, heart shaped foliage and the bright red, trailing stems offer a striking contrast. Trained to a support, the majestic size of the plant with vines up to 20 feet long commands attention.

VARIETIES

Presently malabar red stem is the only variety on the market.

SITE & SOIL REQUIREMENTS

Malabar spinach loves to soak up the sun, so pick a spot that gets plenty of light. Owing to its native habitat, it will tolerate poor soils, but not poor drainage. A little organic matter or sand worked into the soil always helps to facilitate drainage in heavy soils. Compost or rotted manure that is applied at transplant time will also give a nutrient boost to get this green giant off to a jolly good start.

PLANTING

Being a native of warm climates, malabar spinach will balk at germinating in cool soil. Even under the best conditions, germination is only about 50 to 60 percent. It is best to start the plants indoors, 3 to 4 weeks before the last possible frost.

Place the seeds in a moist starting mix and cover with ¼ inch of the mix. Keep moist and warm, about 75°F, until the first set of true leaves develops. At this stage, each tiny plant can be transplanted into individual 2¼-inch pots.

Be sure to harden off the plants before setting into the garden. Transplant them at the same depth that they grew in their individual containers, and set them 12 to 18 inches apart. Set them in a straight line to trellis on a fence or up an A frame, or circle some around a tepee-style trellis (see illustrations on pages 21 to 23 and pages 26 to 27).

Direct seeding is possible in warm weather. Sow 5 or 6 seeds in hills that are placed 12 to 18 inches apart. Cover with ¼ to ½ inch of fine soil, and keep moist until they sprout. Once the seedlings are growing well, thin to the best one in each hill.

TRELLISING

Malabar spinach is a vigorous, climbing vine that grows by twining its stem around a support. Twine, wire, poles, or fence-type frames are all suitable (see illustrations on pages 22 and 23). Be sure that whatever you use is sturdy enough to support the weight of the vines. Set up the trellis before transplant time to avoid any disruption of the plants' roots. The trailing stems may need a little initial guidance in finding their support. By gently leaning them against the lower levels of the trellis, they should grow in the right direction.

GROWING TIPS
Although it loves the heat, malabar spinach is a fleshy-leafed plant and requires plenty of water. Check the plants often and never let the soil dry out completely. Mulch to conserve water and to hold down weeds.

This plant's tolerance for weak soil makes it easy to grow without much thought of fertilizing. You cannot go wrong, though, with an occasional top dressing of compost or rotted manure.

As the seemingly endless vines grow on, you may want to head them back, or they will start to resemble something from a late-night, horror film. Even if you continuously snip a bit here and there to supplement your summer greens, this plant is so productive that you may never be able to tell where cuttings were taken.

PESTS & DISEASES
This is one of those rare and welcome plants that has been grown nearly pest and disease free.

RIPE & READY
Plants are mature enough to endure a little harvesting by the time that they are 2 to 3 feet tall. Cut off the tender new shoots for salads, or pluck the leaves and serve them either fresh in salads or as cooked greens. Like most greens, summer spinach is rich in calcium, and the red stems are good sources of fiber and vitamin A.

BEANS
Beans have long been a traditional favorite among home gardeners. Not only are they easy to plant and grow, but also they benefit the soil. Like all legumes, beans have the ability to extract nitrogen from the air and convert it into a form that is usable and accessible by plants. This is accomplished with the help of soil-dwelling microorganisms that adhere to the roots of the plants and transform the molecules of nitrogen from their gaseous state in the soil into nitrogen-containing solids that the plant roots can absorb. With nitrogen as one of the three most heavily utilized elements of all green growing plants, this is no small claim to fame.

Many types of legumes are used as cover crops solely for this valuable benefit, but anyone who has ever savored the fresh flavor of beans, just plucked from the vine, lightly steamed and buttered, knows there are even more enjoyable rewards. As a group, beans are easy to grow and often produce bumper crops over a long season. They may be used or preserved in a variety of ways with healthful, satisfying results. Pole beans, while generally bearing a little later than bush varieties, make up for their late start with extended harvests, bigger beans, and a more "beany" taste.

VARIETIES

Pole beans come in a delightful array of colors, sizes, textures, and flavors. Snap beans range from reliable shades of green to creamy gold or brash purple. Romano beans are broad, tender beans with a distinctive flavor. Lima beans, also called butter beans, come in both large and "baby" types. There are even novelty beans, such as the asparagus or yard-long variety, that, while tender and tasty if picked under 18 inches in length, can grow to gargantuan proportions.

SITE & SOIL REQUIREMENTS

Although beans are not fussy plants, they do have their preferences. Like many cultivated plants, they prefer a sunny spot and well-drained soil. Do not plant them where water pools after a rain. If the soil has a drainage problem, correct this by incorporating sand or organic matter, such as peat, compost, or rotted manure. Beans favor a humus-rich soil, but beware of too much nitrogen; it can prompt plants to produce excess vines and leaves and fewer, later bean pods.

Soil should be well worked and friable to a depth of 12 to 18 inches and be slightly acidic. A pH range from 5.5 to 6.5 is ideal.

Beans simply will not tolerate cold feet. Except for fava beans, a cool growing cousin, beans demand warm soil. Lima beans will not consider germinating in soil temperatures less than 65°F. Experiment with a soil warming technique by laying black or clear plastic over the prepared soil several weeks prior to planting. Turning in half-rotted compost a few weeks before planting is another heat-generating trick. And for those sophisticates not to be outdone by humble bean seeds, you can always have heating cables installed underneath your bean beds!

PLANTING

Plant beans after all danger of frost is past, and the soil has begun to warm. While a planting depth of 1 inch is commonly recommended, poking the seeds down 2 inches may give a little added insurance against an odd, cool night. Space seeds 2 or 3 inches apart, and leave enough room between rows or groups for you to work. Press the soil down gently, but firmly, and soak.

Plant lima bean seeds with the "eye" spot facing down. This is where the first roots will emerge and will orient the young plant in the right direction.

Pole bean seeds will germinate in 7 to 14 days or sooner if presprouted. Presprouting may help you get a jump on a short growing season. Place bean seeds in a wet coffee filter or paper towel. Fold and place in a plastic bag, and let sit in a windowsill for 2 days. Check carefully for roots to emerge. The germinating seeds must be handled with extreme care because any damage or bruising will injure the infant plant. After the seeds have sprouted, follow outdoor planting directions. Never try starting bean plants indoors because they detest transplanting and will express their displeasure by growing into weak plants with sad harvests.

One of the best things that you can do for your bean crop, especially if you are planting in a spot where no legumes have grown before, is to inoculate the seeds with soft, black powder. The powder, or inoculate, is thousands of microbes that convert nitrogen from a gas into a usable form. Since some soils may be lacking in these organisms, it is prudent to insure their presence by pretreating your seeds. The inoculate is available through garden outlets or mail-order catalogues.

Treating seeds is quick and easy. Empty the contents of the inoculate packet into a jar or sealable, plastic bag, toss in the seeds (first soak the seeds overnight), and gently shake until the seeds are well coated.

TRELLISING

Beans will twine around anything! Ten-foot bean poles that are driven into the soil have long been a common sight in backyard gardens. But there are so many other ways.

Another very popular method for training pole beans is to plant around a tepee. Especially in windy areas, it is a good idea to push the bottom ends of the poles into the soil for stability. Position the poles in a 3-foot-wide circle and leave about 6 inches between the foot of each pole. One or two vines can climb each leg of the tepee. A running tepee is also superb for pole beans. Space the feet of the poles from 6 to 10 inches apart. (See tepee illustrations on page 21.)

Fence-type trellises are also great for beans. Twine or wire supports serve equally well on a fence or an A frame (see illustrations on pages 22 and 23 and pages 26 and 27). The slight slant of the A frame allows the beans to hang down away from the foliage, which makes them a snap to pick. Commercial bean towers work fine, but for the price, you can construct enough trellises for every vine in the garden.

The most important thing to consider when choosing a trellis for pole beans is that it be tall enough for 8 foot or longer vines. It is also important to have the trellis ready before you plant. Any poles or posts that extend beneath the soil line should go into the ground before the seeds. Otherwise, you may accidentally damage tender seedling roots. Once up, the seedlings may need to be placed against their support; but once they latch on, they are on their way.

GROWING TIPS

Beans do not like to be overcrowded. Once the young plants have become established, thin to the best 2 or 3 per pole or 1 vine every 6 inches along a fence. Never pull up the castoffs; their roots may be intertwined with their neighbors. Instead, snip them off with scissors to avoid disturbing other plant roots.

Weed with care to avoid annoying those delicate roots. Cultivate shallowly since the feeder roots are near the surface. Putting down a 4-inch layer of mulch will significantly cut down on any weeding and also will help to keep the roots cool and moist.

Beans require about 1 inch of water per week. Drip irrigation is the best way to provide water. Not only do drip or soaker hoses cut down on wasted water, but also they prevent the foliage from getting splashed. Splashing water is a key mode of disease transmission. Never work around bean plants when they are wet since this is another common way of spreading diseases.

Although beans thrive in 70° to 80°F, hot, dry spells may cause them to close up shop temporarily—they may drop blossoms or bean pods. As soon as the heat lets up, the problem passes.

Enjoy a variety of pole beans. They are self-pollinating, which means you can plant different types side by side along the same bean pole without the possibility of the plants crossing. Most varieties mature in 60 to 65 days, but by planting different kinds, you can be picking beans throughout most of the summer.

PESTS & DISEASES

Unfortunately, beans seem to be just as popular with the insect population as they are with gardeners. Tiny, black bean aphids congregate to suck the juices from tender plant parts. Leafhoppers damage plants both through feeding and spreading the curly top virus; resistant varieties are available and predatory lacewings will help with this problem. A bevy of beetles in larval and adult forms, including spotted bean leaf beetles and Mexican bean beetles, will feed on various parts of the plant. Pick off the larvae and the adults and destroy the eggs. Cutworms topple seedlings, while wireworms cut them off beneath the surface. Seed corn maggots gut the seed as it germinates. Tilling helps to reduce all of these pests.

In stored seed, bean weevils invade the pods, reemerge, and leave large holes in the seed. Heating seed to 135°F for 3 hours will kill any larvae that are present.

Diseases are best prevented by staying out of a wet bean patch and by pulling out and burning any suspicious looking plants. It is important to buy disease-free seed and to choose resistant varieties if diseases have been a problem. Be on guard for anthracnose, a fungus that causes dark, sunken spots; bacterial bean blight that causes large yellow to brown patches on leaves; and common bean mosaic that is frequently spread by aphids and leaves the foliage yellowed and curling and the plants stunted. Bacterial wilt destroys seedlings as does curly top, a virus that is spread by whiteflies and leafhoppers. Powdery mildew causes gray spots and stunted, curling leaves, while downy mildew produces a white mold on lima bean pods. Other fungal diseases include root rot, which affects and destroys the main tap root and seed rot, or damping off, which is characterized by the youngest seedlings toppling over.

RIPE & READY

Beans should be harvested regularly to stimulate continued flower and pod production. For snap beans, this means picking them just as the seeds begin to form within the pods; left too long on the vine, they will become tough. Lima beans should also be picked frequently once the pods begin to swell. To pick bean pods, grasp the vine with one hand and the bean with the other hand, and quickly snap it free. Avoid twisting or damaging the still producing vine.

For shell beans, the harvest is a onetime chore. These beans are left on the plants until they are nearly dry, then pulled and allowed to finish drying in a warm, dry, well-ventilated place. Package the beans in plastic bags, and store in a cool, dry place. Where they are present, bean weevils are the main drawback to this method.

Snap beans can be dehydrated for storage with good results. They are great for freezing and may be pickled or canned, but nothing can compare with eating them fresh from the garden. Fresh green beans are a good source of vitamins A, B_1, B_2, and C, calcium, iron, and fiber. Their flavor and texture are at their peak immediately after picking.

BLACKBERRIES

Sweet, soft, summer memories of deliciously fragrant, wild blackberries, dripping from spiny brambles, inviting yet defying, inspire many nostalgic gardeners to plant a patch to call their own. Domestic versions of those wild vines offer many advantages over those well-remembered thickets, including more and bigger fruit and fewer thorns.

VARIETIES

Perhaps the most striking development in the ole' briar patch is the thornless varieties. Black Satin, Hull, and Thornfree are commonly offered in nursery stores and mail-order catalogues. These cultivars not only offer pain-free fruit, but also are much more cold tolerant than their wild cousins. Their growth habit is erect and forms, if left unchecked, more of an unruly bush than a sprawling network of vines. Erect blackberries are stiff caned and need less support and guidance than the trailing varieties. Although most require a moderate to mild winter chill in order to set fruit the following season, some, such as Humble, were bred specifically for gentle winter climates.

Considerably more tender than the erect blackberries are the trailing varieties that are very familiar to southerners and natives of the Pacific Northwest. Often referred to as Dewberries, this group includes both thornless (Thornless Evergreen) and thorny (Cascade, Aurora) varieties. Marion Berries, Boisen Berries, and Logan Berries are all trailing blackberries that are known by their variety name rather than by Dewberries.

Blackberries are closely related to raspberries, but are more vigorous and productive. Most, however, are not nearly as cold tolerant as their cousins. Gardeners in the extreme north may be frustrated by their blackberries' sensitivity to cold, while those in the deep south must settle for the few varieties that do not require winter's cold to produce dormancy. But for true blackberry lovers in most of the country, the many available varieties of cultivars offer the bonus of a summer full of mouth-watering berries. By including a few each of very early, early, midseason, and late ripening varieties in the blackberry patch, you can enjoy fresh blackberries all season.

SITE & SOIL REQUIREMENTS

Be careful when choosing a site for blackberries. They require full sun, and when in full vine, they will shade other nearby plants. If not properly maintained, they will spread prolifically. Never start blackberries where solanaceous crops (tomatoes, potatoes, eggplant, or peppers) have previously grown because the soil may harbor verticillium wilt, and the vines will not grow.

Blackberries produce deep root systems that make them intolerant of shallow, heavy soils. Deep, light soil with good drainage is perfect. Adequate moisture retention is also essential since these plants generally ripen their juicy crop during the driest part of the season. Soil that is well amended with organic matter provides both the desired texture and the water drainage and retention that is so necessary to healthy, productive vines.

Blackberries favor a slightly acid soil (pH 6.5 to 6.8). You can maintain this pH range and boost soil, nutrient levels by providing moderate applications of rotted horse manure every other year.

PLANTING

Plants that are available through nursery catalogues or stores are generally 1- or 2-year-old bare-root canes. They can be transplanted early in the spring, 3 to 4 weeks before the last expected frost.

When planting, keep the roots moist until ready to set out. Dig a hole

12 to 18 inches deep and wide enough to accommodate the bundle of roots. Position each plant so that the crown is just at the soil level or very slightly below. Fill the hole part way with a combination of top soil and added organic matter, such as rotted manure or compost. Water deeply and let the water absorb into the soil around the plant roots. Fill in the hole and water again. The plants should be set 3 to 5 feet apart in rows 8 feet apart. The bushy, erect varieties need a little extra spacing to allow for cultivation and harvest. After the canes are set into the ground, prune them to a length of 6 to 10 inches.

TRELLISING

Blackberries do not exactly climb; they sprawl in all directions. While it is entirely possible to grow masses of blackberry vines without trellising, doing this is an open invitation to a garden takeover. Most vines sucker very easily and spread at an amazing rate. Untamed mountains of tangled, spiny vines can be harvested to some degree by wading in with high boots and protective clothing and by throwing down a plank as a portable pathway. Vines that are allowed to sprawl hardly offer the easiest pickings nor the best fruit and are much more subject to pests, diseases, and the breakage that accompanies those boots and planks.

Erect blackberries, while touted by the garden mail-order catalogues as "needing no support," fare much better with at least a little guidance. Set up a clothesline trellis (see illustration on page 23) with a wire on either side of the bushes to hold them in place. You may tie the canes to the wires or simply allow them to grow within their limits.

Trailing varieties can be trained to any type of trellis that suits your needs. A simple, double-stranded, fence-type trellis serves well. As the vines grow, loop or zigzag them along the wires. Tie with soft cord at intervals, and position the vines so that they receive maximum sunlight and air flow. The vines can also be trained onto a wire mesh, fence-type trellis or up the sloping sides of an A frame (see illustrations on pages 23, 26, and 27).

GROWING TIPS

Blackberries are perennial plants that send out biennial vines. This means that each vine lives for 2 years. It grows the first year and sprouts buds at the end of that season; it sets fruit during the second year. The vines arc incredibly susceptible to pests and diseases. As soon as a cane has borne fruit and has been harvested, it should be cut to the ground, removed, and burned.

A heavy mulch can minimize two serious blackberry problems; it will help conserve previous moisture and keep weeds down. This is especially important since weeds can harbor insects or diseases, and cultivation can disrupt temperamental roots and cause suckers to form. A thick mulch can also help to prevent frostbite if winter temperatures dip too low. Some varieties are so tender that the vines must be taken down and buried under several inches of soil to prevent winterkill.

The readiness of suckers to form does have one positive aspect. If you ever wish to move or expand your blackberry patch, allow the suckers to grow and transplant them at your convenience. Some trailing blackberries may be "tipped" toward the end of the season. Tipped means that if a vine is allowed to outgrow the confines of the trellis, it will bend to the ground and take root. You can guide these tips to root in prepared, ground level containers and cut them from the parent plant as soon as the roots become established. While propagating blackberries from established plants is easy, it is not always simple. Be sure your berries are not a protected or patented variety before starting new plants; it is illegal to propagate any such plants.

PESTS & DISEASES

The two most important things that you can do to prevent insects or disease from ruining your blackberries are to keep your own patch immaculate and to destroy any wild counterparts in the vicinity. Memories aside, those free ranging brambles are often plagued with diseases and bugs, not to mention Brier Rabbit. Even related plants, such as apple or cherry trees or your prize rose bushes, will share their ailments with your blackberries.

Bird netting or scare devices will discourage feathered thieves. An under leaf dose of rotenone should stop spider mites, the leaf greedy larvae of the blackberry sawfly, and May beetles. Pick off leaves that are infested with leaf miners to slow their progress. Odd growth and swollen galls in canes are the work of cane borers. Removing and burning the egg filled galls will prevent a new generation from emerging. Other pests that attack blackberries include the mostly harmless blackberry psyllid, flaky rose scale, and cane-girdling tree crickets.

Blackberries are quite susceptible to anthracnose, which begins as purplish welts and advances to falling leaves and berries and splitting, dying canes. Good air circulation can help reduce the chances of spreading this and other fungal diseases, such as septoria leaf spot or the flower-deforming, fruit-preventing, double blossom.

Orange rust is also a serious disease. Once detected, the only remedy is to dig up and destroy infected plants before the disease spreads. Crown gall produces galls on the roots that ultimately weaken or kill the plants. Stunted plants may be the result of a dwarfing virus, commonly called rosette. A number of viruses afflict blackberries, and your best defense is to insist on certified, virus-free stock when you buy your berry plants.

RIPE & READY

From 1 to 3 years after blackberry vines are planted, they should be handsomely rewarding you with buckets of mouth-watering, finger-staining berries. Trellising makes the picking a much easier, less time-consuming task. Even if you are harvesting thorny plants, you will not need any special, protective gear other than a pair of garden gloves. Make a berry bucket by punching two holes in the top of a coffee can or other serviceable container and running a piece of twine or wire through the holes. Pass one end of the twine through your belt loop before feeding it back through the holes to free your hands for picking.

Just as the glossy blackberries begin to lose their shine, they are ready to be harvested. When truly ripe, they will drop at the slightest touch. They are very easily bruised and should be transferred periodically from your berry basket to a shallow container. The best time to pick is early in the morning just after the dew has burned off, but before the temperature begins to rise.

Blackberries are wonderful in pies, cobblers, jams, syrups, and home-made wines. Most varieties freeze very well. Fresh, they are a good source of phosphorus, calcium, magnesium, and vitamin A.

CUCUMBERS

Why do we say "cool as a cucumber" when cucumbers detest anything less than warm, dry, summer days? Cool weather puts them in a slump; they will not grow, they will not set fruit, and many succumb to disease. They are not that finicky to grow, however, if their sensitive nature is respected.

Just give them good weather, plenty of water, and a stress-free life, and they will produce more crispy, dark green picklers and slicers than you will know what to do with!

VARIETIES

Traditionally, cucumbers have been divided into two types: small, crisp varieties for pickling and larger, mild tasting fruits for slicing and fresh eating. Excellent cultivars, many resistant to disease, are available in both categories.

Some cucumber plants are gynoecious and produce only female (fruiting) flowers. These plants bear heavier yields than monoecious (produce male and female flowers) varieties, but they still must be pollinated. Nurseries always include a male-flowering pollinator variety to ensure that fruit sets. You can identify which flowers are male and which are female by looking for a tiny bulge behind the blossom that looks like a miniature cucumber; only the female flowers have them. There are even parthenocarpic (seedless hybrids) that require no pollination and can be grown pest free under crop covers until harvest.

If you enjoy the flavor of cucumbers, but they do not agree with you, try growing one of the many "burpless" varieties, such as Sweet Slice or Euro-American Hybrids. Exotic looking, but deliciously mild and sweet, Armenian cucumbers may grow to 2 to 3 feet long. There are also oriental varieties and a variety called Lemon that resembles its namesake in size and color, but has a unique flavor all its own.

SITE & SOIL REQUIREMENTS

Cucumbers like full sun and lots of it. It is also important not to plant them where previous cucumbers or related plants, such as squash, pumpkins, or melons, have grown within the last 3 years. Diseases common to all can hide out in the soil for at least 1 or 2 years.

Cucumbers flourish in soils high in organic matter and nutrients. They prefer a well-worked, slightly acid (pH 6.5 to 7), well-drained soil.

PLANTING

These vines may either be started indoors or directly seeded. Be forewarned, however, cucumbers and their relatives do not like to be transplanted.

Once the soil is well warmed (70°F), you can plant or transplant cucumbers. Dig 2 inches of compost into the soil, or add a weak, well-balanced fertilizer (5-10-5) to get them off to a running start. Mound the soil into a hill, or plant in raised beds. The raised soil warms faster and drains well; two things cucumbers really appreciate.

To seed directly, sow seeds ½ to 1 inch deep, 4 to 6 inches apart. Lightly press down the soil, and water well. They will germinate in 7 to 14 days.

To start cucumbers indoors, wait until 3 to 4 weeks before the last frost. Although cucumbers resent any sort of disruption, especially the stress of transplanting, you can minimize the aggravation by using peat pots. Grow the seedlings on a sunny windowsill or under lights until they are ready to set out into the garden. Then set the plants, pots and all, into the ground so that the entire container is well covered with soil. A transplant solution, such as a weak fish emulsion, will give the seedlings a boost.

SETTING OUT PEAT OR FIBER POTS

When planting seedlings or plants grown in peat or fiber pots, be sure that the pots are thoroughly soaked. Tear off the bottoms of the pots to encourage the plant's roots to grow.

TRELLISING

Cucumbers really benefit from trellising. They are extremely susceptible to diseases that are brought on by high humidity and poor air circulation that is typical of grounded vines. Oddly misshapen fruits are also the product of grounded vines. Cucumbers produce straight fruit, however, when hanging from a support.

Cucumbers climb by tightly coiling tendrils, but a soft tie here and there will keep them in the right place, especially on a vertical trellis. Fence-type trellises with wire mesh for plant support work well for cucumbers (see illustration on page 23). A frames, pipe, and wooden lattice designs have also been used with good results. Some gardeners caution that wire or metal may overheat and burn the tendrils or leaves, but the leaves should shade the frame well enough to prevent this. Wire or pipe can be wrapped with florists' tape to prevent it from burning the vines.

The zigzag series of A frame trellises is very popular for cucumbers. It is easily relocated year after year to facilitate crop rotation, and cucumbers find the sloping sides easy to scale (see illustration on page 27).

Cucumbers are shallow rooted and can be damaged when a trellis is anchored into the ground. Set the trellis up at or before transplant time to avoid harming the roots.

GROWING TIPS

Shallow roots mean cucumbers are thirsty plants. Mulching them will help. Commercial growers recommend using plastic sheeting because it warms the soil and stops weeds as well as conserves moisture. Drip irrigation is great for cucumbers because it eliminates the waste and potential disease transmission of splashing water. If you do irrigate with a sprinkler, do it in the morning so that the foliage can dry during the day. An alternative to expensive drip systems or soaker hoses is to sink a container into the soil at planting time. Punch a few holes in a gallon milk jug, old bucket, or other container, and fill with water. The water will slowly drain out at root level.

If direct seeded, thin to 1 plant every 12 inches by snipping out all but the best vines; pulling culls can stress the roots of the remaining plants. Keep transplants, though, covered at night for the first few weeks to protect them from any unexpected dip in temperature.

As the vines begin to flower, apply a top dressing of organic fertilizer to give them a boost as they set fruit. In plants that produce both male and female flowers, often the first blooms to appear are fruitless males, which soon drop off the vine. Remember, only female flowers set fruit. To do this, however, they must receive pollen from male flowers and this depends on insects—primarily bees. If your vines are not fruiting, you can give nature a hand by doing the job yourself. Pluck the petals from a male flower, and rub the pollen covered anthers gently around the inside of a female blossom. The pollen will adhere to the sticky stigma, work its way to the blossom's ovaries, and soon a cucumber is born!

Different cucumber varieties can cross-pollinate, but this affects only the next generation of seeds not the current season's harvest. Related vine crops, such as squash and melons, do not cross with cucumbers.

Anything that you can do to make your cucumbers' lives easier will be repaid at the harvest. Anything that stresses them can cause off tasting, bitter fruit. Be sure plants are hardened off before transplanting. Do not cultivate near the roots, and protect them from frost and insects. Do not let them go thirsty. After all this attention, your cucumber vines should reward you generously.

PESTS & DISEASES

Drape an insect-proof row cover over your cucumber plants, and forget about many of the harmful bugs. Just be sure to remove the covers for pollination. Or, you can pollinate the plants by hand or select a variety that sets fruit without pollination.

Aphids can be squished or blasted off with cold water. Cucumber beetles come in striped and spotted varieties that feed on the plants and transmit diseases; radishes planted nearby may help repel them. Stinky squash bugs poke tiny holes along the vines, but tend to avoid trellised plants. Vine borers chew an opening into the vine at ground level and digest the insides of the stems. Upwardly mobile vines offer far fewer entry points, and an injectable bacteria, *Bacillus thuringiensis* (Bt), will stop the bores.

Anthracnose affects cucumbers first as small, dark spots that run together and later as moldy or dropping fruit; crop rotation is essential in preventing it. Downy mildew causes downy purple spots on leaves that may eventually lead to the death of the leaves or the entire plant. Bacterial wilt causes an apparently healthy vine to wilt so suddenly that the leaves still look healthy; cucumber beetles spread this lethal surprise, so keep them in check. Mosaic virus stunts plant growth and causes yellow leaves and malformed fruit. Prevent these and other cucumber diseases by following the three-year-rotation rule of not planting cucumbers where previous, related plants were grown and by keeping all garden debris, especially any sick plants, cleaned up. Also, whenever possible, choose disease-resistant varieties.

RIPE & READY

The mild crunch of fresh cucumbers is hard to beat in a summer salad. Although not terribly nutritious, they do provide a good dose of dietary fiber and, if the skins are left on, vitamins A and C.

Cucumbers are not ripened on the vine unless you want to save the seeds. A vine ripened cucumber is yellow and hard with large, well-developed seeds. If not kept picked while the fruits are green, the vine will stop producing. Harvest often to encourage further production. Cucumbers can be picked at any size past 2 inches long, although most are best if picked before they reach 10 inches in length or 1½ inches in diameter. Armenian cucumbers are still of good quality when they are over 2 feet long and up to 2½ inches thick. While picklers are picked when small and very tender, the perfect slicer has a dark, glossy, green skin with firm, crisp flesh and measures from 6 to 10 inches long.

Cucumbers are refreshing when they are sliced or chunked and wonderful in a fresh green or Greek salad. Pickle recipes abound for everything from the tiniest, sweet gherkins to super dills and chunky, bread-and-butter pickles.

GRAPES

One of the undisputed stars of any garden is the grapevine. From beautiful foliage that will quickly grow to provide a privacy screen to bunches of sweet, juicy grapes, it has so much to offer. Since grapes are particular about their growing conditions and take up to three years to produce fruit, many gardeners do not think they are worth the effort. But to reach up and pluck a perfectly ripe, sugary sweet, homegrown grape from your arbor and pop it into your mouth is to be converted forever!

VARIETIES

Grapes are one of the oldest, cultivated plants and have been altered tremendously from their wild state. From a handful of native plants, thousands of varieties have been developed.

There are various distinctions between different types of grapes. Table grapes differ from wine grapes; they are sweeter and tastier straight from the vine. There are regular seeded and seedless varieties and red, white, and blue types with a fabulous range of tastes. Muscadine grapes are different from other types. They require special pruning and trellising techniques, but offer a great variety of colors and flavors in return. Many muscadine vines require cross-pollination to set fruit, unlike most grapes which are self-pollinating. The vast majority of grapevines, however, will set fruit even if they are the only grapes in the garden.

Some varieties of table grapes that you may wish to try could include the white grapes: Seneca, Golden Muscat, Niagara, Himrod, and Remaily; red varieties: Catawba, Suffolk Red Seedless, and Reliance Seedless; and the true blue Concord. Wine grapes that you may associate with your favorite vintner's label might include Cabernet Sauvignon, Chardonnay, Chenin Blanc, French Colombard, Pinot Noir, and Zinfandel. All of these grapes are tremendously dependent on just the right environment. Do not expect your crop to mirror the best of ancient, French vineyards. Just enjoy growing, experimenting, and improving the bounty of your vines.

Ask your local nursery owner for help in choosing varieties for your garden and try at least three or four suggestions; they will not take up much space when they are trained along trellises. Not only will you enjoy a variety of colors and tastes, but also you are sure to find that some types do not agree with your plot, while you will hopefully discover a precious few that will thrive.

SITE & SOIL REQUIREMENTS

Certain combinations of terrain, soil, and climate are more suited to grape growing than others. This is why some areas of the world are renowned as "Grape Country." Although soil preferences differ somewhat among varieties, grapes are not dependent on rich, fertile soil. Some of the most successful vineyards in the world have been maintained for generations on weak-soiled, rock strewn slopes. Even though the vines will take root and grow in nearly any kind of soil, most prefer a light, gravelly loam. They will do well in heavier soils, even clay, as long as there is sufficient gravel or rock to facilitate drainage. With roots that extend to 8 feet deep and more, grapevines demand good drainage and deep soil. Stones or gravel in the soil also help to hold heat during cool, fall days.

Oddly, soils high in organic matter and nutrients can be detrimental to a grape crop. The vines tend to grow profusely, but the woody parts do not mature, and fruit production is low and often of inferior quality.

Besides drainage, the most important aspect of your potential grape-growing soil is the site that it occupies. Grapes are hillbillies. They love a gentle slope and prefer to face the southeast or southwest, especially when they are grown in northern gardens. Some type of windbreak, such as a stand of trees at the base of the slope, helps moderate windchill. Flat plots are frowned upon by the vines because such places are subject to unexpected frosts and still, stagnate air that may promote fungal diseases. Sunken areas are even worse and usually have poor drainage.

The other chief concern of the grapevine's location is the area's climate.

New cultivars constantly are being introduced for northern gardeners, and some are hardy to -30°F. Most grapes, however, luxuriate in long, lazy summers and warm autumns. They may suffer if winter temperatures dip below zero, or if they are caught by a late spring or early fall freeze.

PLANTING

The gardener who sets out his or her new grapevines is committing an act of faith. The most important part of home, grape growing has already been done—the very best variety or varieties for the plot have been selected. The site has been picked, hopefully on a slope, but at least in full sun. The best that can be done now is to get this newcomer off to a good start.

Begin by thoroughly working the soil as deeply as possible. You may want to add some organic matter, sand, or gravel to improve drainage. Once the soil is prepared, dig a hole deep enough and wide enough to accommodate the root mass. Be sure that while you are working, the roots are kept moist. Before setting the vine into the hole, cut away any damaged roots, and prune the roots to about 10 inches long. Choose the strongest, best looking cane that rises from the crown to be the central leader for the vine, and remove all the others. The central leader will be the trunk of the new grapevine. It, too, needs to be trimmed back to 2 or 3 healthy buds.

Set the fledgling vine into the hole, and add a few inches of good, garden soil. Holding the plant near the crown, gently tug upward to let the soil settle around the roots. Fill in the hole, and give the plant a good soaking. Once the water has drained, press the soil firmly, and add more soil if necessary.

Since most varieties are self-pollinating, you can plant only one. If planting two or more, space them about 8 feet apart or 10 to 12 feet apart for muscadine varieties. Planting grapes is a springtime job and is best completed while the plants are dormant or just beginning to form buds; they will then have months of comparably mild weather to become established before having to face the winter.

TRELLISING

Grapes are often pictured sprawling over an arbor for a wonderfully dramatic effect (see illustration on page 28). The spreading vines should be trained and tied along horizontal supports. Design the arbor so that the supports are sturdy enough not only to hold up the bearing vines, but also the tending gardener. Once established, a grape arbor makes an unparalleled, garden retreat. It may take two or three years for the trunk to reach the top of the arbor. While it is in training, you will have to keep removing any side shoots. Once it reaches its intended height, allow the vines to fan out over the arbor, and train accordingly.

The traditional method for growing grapes is to train the vine along a wire, fence-type trellis (see illustration on page 23). Heavy 9- or 10-gauge wire must be strung tightly and kept taut under the weight of branches and fruit. Turnbuckles connected to one end of the wire and to an eyebolt set into an end post can be adjusted to maintain the wire tension. Some growers suggest using copper wire for supports not only because of its strength and durability, but also because copper is a main ingredient in antifungal sprays that are used routinely to battle grape diseases.

You will also need sturdy posts, at least 4 inches in diameter, to construct a grape trellis. These posts will be under considerable stress from the tension of the wire and the weight of the vines. Bury 8-foot posts, 2 feet deep, or use longer posts and bury them even deeper. You can make the posts more solid by anchoring them in concrete and/or by bracing each end post with a 4x4 post that is wedged into the ground. End posts will bear most of the load and must be the sturdiest. Intermediate posts should be set between every 3 vines or along every 24 feet of trellis. Heavy-duty metal fence posts may be substituted for wooden ones, but must be well braced.

Regional climate and the variety of grape will dictate the type of trellis and training method that you should use. Three well-tested methods are called the Kniffen, Fan, and Modified Chautauqua systems. These can be manipulated to suit different hardiness zones for most grape varieties. Muscadine and a few other wine grapes require a different technique called a Single T, which promotes short, vertical branches to form along the main horizontal arms.

The Kniffen system is commonly used in areas with temperatures of -20°F or above. The trellis consists of two wires that are strung between posts. Some growers use a heavier gauge wire (Number 9) for the upper wire and a somewhat lighter gauge (Number 10) along the bottom. The bottom wire should be strung 30 inches from the ground and stapled firmly to the posts. The upper wire is 24 to 30 inches above the lower wire.

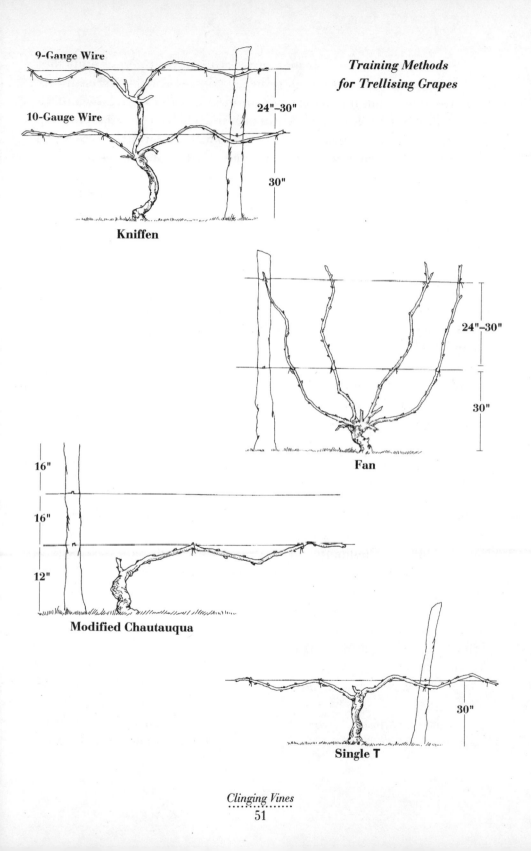

9-Gauge Wire

10-Gauge Wire

24"–30"

30"

Kniffen

*Training Methods
for Trellising Grapes*

24"–30"

30"

Fan

16"

16"

12"

Modified Chautauqua

30"

Single T

The vines are trained gradually over a three-year period until four arms, or cordons, extend from the central leader—one following each wire away from the trunk. In the first year, the vine is allowed to grow until it reaches the lowest strand of wire, and the top of the vine is tied to it. It will continue to grow up to the top wire. As it reaches this point, the vine is tied in place, and the growing end is snipped. In the following spring, the pruning continues before the buds begin to swell. As the vine grows, choose four side branches to train along the wires, and clip off any others as they form.

In the vine's third season, select another set of four vines to train. The fruit of the vine will form along the arms that grew the season before, and the new branches will be trained in their place after the harvest to produce fruit the next year. Keep all other shoots pinched back, and after the harvest, which will be slight the very first time, remove the four old vines. Tie the new branches in their place, and keep all extra shoots, or suckers, trimmed. This process of training four vines and allowing a new set of four to grow will continue every year for up to a half century with full, grape production commencing after the third year.

Growers in less temperate zones where winter temperatures can dip to -30° to -40°F may choose a Fan or Modified Chautauqua system. Either of these methods allows for protecting low growing trunks against temperature extremes. The Fan system employs the same post and wire trellis as the Kniffen, but in a different manner. In the Fan system, the main leader is kept to only 12 inches high. Four or five canes are allowed to sprout and are tied to the wires in a spreading fan pattern. Each year another set of 4 or 5 new vines is allowed to develop as successors.

The Modified Chautauqua uses a three-wire trellis with the first wire strung 12 inches from the ground and the other two wires at 16-inch intervals. Here, too, the central leader is kept short. Developing canes are trained up onto the wires. After the growing season, the entire grapevine is untied and buried under 6 to 8 inches of soil to protect the vines from the winter cold. The stubby trunk can be protected by mounding dirt against it. Most cold damage to grapevines is sustained in the main stems. These methods, however, give the grower a good chance against the ravages of winter.

Muscadine and many wine grapes set fruit along short vertical shoots or spurs that rise up from the horizontal cordons rather than along the cordons themselves; therefore, these must be trained in a slightly different way—the Single T method. The Single T trellis is constructed like previously discussed methods, but with only a single wire that is strung about 30 inches from the ground. The central leader is trained up to the wire as before, and a strong vine is allowed to grow from either side. These side branches are grown longer than in the other training methods to accommodate as many vertical shoots as the plant can sustain. These shoots, or spurs, are pruned to 2 or 3 buds, each of which will produce a cluster of grapes in the fall. After they produce, the spurs are pruned to make way for those that will bear the following year.

Vine pruning should be done when the plant is dormant or nearly dormant. Any time after the leaves fall in the autumn until the buds begin to swell the next spring is fine. Do not prune, however, when the wood is frozen since brittle canes are easily broken or damaged. Pruning cuts should be made about 1 inch past the last bud to be saved. During the growing season, keep an eye on the vines to see how productive each one is. Clusters that grow too thick or close together deplete the reserves of the plant and are susceptible to rot and diseases. An overabundance of fruit can be thinned from the vines at any stage.

GROWING TIPS

Grapes really need little attention other than training and pruning. They may benefit from a gentle feeding of compost just before they set fruit. If soil is truly weak, and the plants fail to grow or foliage turns yellow, an organic, nitrogen fertilizer may be called for.

Good air circulation is a real boon to bearing grapevines. Pests and disease organisms take refuge in the dense, moist canopy of the leafy vines. Although leaves are essential to the health of the plant and produce food from sunlight and shield developing fruit from its intensity, lush dense layers of leaves also create the perfect microclimate for fungal diseases. Experiments have shown that by thinning a few leaves in the thickest areas, the improved air circulation not only cuts down on disease, but also boosts fruit production and ripening.

Regardless of the method of training used, grapevines only set fruit on one-year-old wood; there must always be a few, new vines growing to replace those in production. Most grapevines can reasonably sustain from 6 to 8 branches, but too much growth or fruit production overtaxes the vine. Reduced yields and poor quality fruit will result. Keep extra shoots trimmed, and remove any branches that do not set fruit along with the others. They may try to set fruit later, but will probably not have time to ripen their load before frost. Dead or diseased vines must be promptly removed.

PESTS & DISEASES

Grapes fall victim to a staggering number of pests, from birds and animals to what seems like most of the insect world. Most are nonspecific or general feeders that are merely taking advantage of whatever fare they find—grapes included. Some pests concentrate on grapes almost exclusively. Be on the lookout for leaves or fruit that show obvious insect activity, such as red or purple spots on fruit or leaves, or those that show evidence of leaf miners or leaf rollers. Remove and burn any such discoveries immediately.

Stop birds with netting that is placed over the vines before the fruit begins to sweeten. Or staple small, brown paper bags over individual bunches of grapes; this is also a good way to stop marauding animals. Grapeberry moths, grape leafhoppers, grape phylloxera, grape sawflies, and Japanese beetles are among those that feed on tasty grape leaves. Grape cane girdlers and tree crickets damage the vines, and rose chafer beetles, yellow jackets, and grape curculio will try to beat you to the feast of fruit.

Grapevines are also susceptible to nematodes—those soil bound threads of garden grief. They feed on the roots and weaken the plant, which opens the door to disease. If nematodes are present in your soil, plant only those grape varieties that are resistant.

Black rot starts as fast growing, light-colored patches on grapes and results in premature raisins that house the spores for the next wave of the disease. Unlike most plant diseases, black rot can be battled by incorporating diseased grapes into the compost heap and then by spreading the finished product along the grapevines to boost their immunity. Dead-arm is another fungal ill that ultimately results in the death of afflicted branches. Both powdery and downy mildew and anthracnose are also common ailments of these noble vines.

Many fungal diseases threaten grapevines. Good air circulation is one of the best preventative tactics to inhibit the growth of debilitating fungi.

Choosing grape varieties that are resistant to fungal diseases is also a wise step in avoiding future disappointment.

RIPE & READY

Since there are so many varieties of grapes, the best rule for harvesting is taste. Even when grapes look ripe, the sugar content may not be fully matured. Only a taste test will tell. Grapes that fail to develop enough sugar to taste sweet may indicate an overburdened vine. Prune the vine drastically, and leave only the choicest branches to bear the following season. Fruit thinning after the clusters have formed will help to balance and lighten the load on the plant. If grapes fail to color, try pinching off a few shading leaves so that they receive more sunlight.

Grapes are harvested by the cluster. Gently snap or snip the stem from the vine to free the bunch. Pick only those that are ripe because they will not improve off the vine. A typical grapevine can be expected to yield up to 15 pounds of fruit per year, and the uses for these grapes are nothing short of legendary. From homemade juices and wines to jellies and syrups, the range of colors and flavors offers an endless variety of rich rewards. Indulge yourself with bunches of fresh table grapes on a warm summer's eve, or dry them into sweet, chewy raisins. Fresh, they are best when refrigerated in perforated plastic bags; they will keep for about two weeks. Dried, they will be delicious for months.

When pruning the vine, do not be too quick to cast out the thinnings, unless, of course, they are diseased. The culled vines are very popular for crafts and are often braided into wreaths or other projects.

HARDY KIWIS

Here is truly an underappreciated fruit. Hardy kiwis have it all. The nutritious fruit is up to twenty times higher in vitamin C than oranges. Unlike the more familiar supermarket kiwis, hardy kiwis are fuzz-free with edible skins. The vines are so decorative with shiny, green foliage and fragrant, white spring blossoms that they can be grown for their landscape value alone. They are hardy to zone 3, grow well in either sun or shade, and are nearly pest and disease free. Once established, a hardy kiwi vine will provide you with beauty and bounty for years.

VARIETIES

Two varieties are readily available through mail-order catalogues. Arctic Beauty is valued for its striking foliage of deep green tipped with bright, contrasting pink and white. Most often grown as an ornamental, it also produces sweet, delicious fruit. It is an early bearer and often produces fruit the first year after planting. Hardy kiwi plants are either female or male. Only the female plants produce fruit, but the males of this variety boast the more dazzling display of color.

Issai is the variety that is more often chosen for its fruit. Vigorous, self-pollinating vines sport an abundance of glossy leaves throughout the season with deliciously scented, white blossoms in the spring. This variety commonly sets luscious, sweet, bite-sized fruit in the season after it is planted—a welcome contrast to those fuzzy relatives that require 3 to 4 years of subtropical weather to produce fruit.

SITE & SOIL REQUIREMENTS

Give 'em sun, give 'em shade—they will give you handfuls of yummy, little kiwis. The number one requirement for these very unfussy vines is that the soil be well drained. They can forgive weak soils, but not wet feet. Sandy soils are especially well tolerated, but those rich in organic matter are best because they provide the necessary drainage and plenty of nutrients.

PLANTING

Vines are usually shipped as bare-root plants and are occasionally available potted. Plant in the spring as you would any bare-root plant (see Blackberries, page 39). Issai can be planted as a single vine, or several can be planted, spaced 10 feet apart. For varieties that are not self-pollinating to set fruit, one male plant must be planted for every eight bearing females within a 100-foot radius.

TRELLISING

Although you may get away with weak soil for hardy kiwis, you will not get off so easily on trellis materials. These stout vines are vigorous and heavy; do not skimp on the building materials. Hardy kiwis also grow very quickly, so have the trellis in place at planting time.

A clothesline trellis is most often recommended (see illustration on page

23). Sink a pair of 8 to 10 foot posts, 4 to 6 inches thick, to a depth of at least 2 feet, about 16 feet apart, with the vine centered in the middle. Anchor the posts by bracing or setting in cement. Attach a heavy-duty, 3-foot-long crossarm on top of each post, and secure three strands of 8- to 12-gauge wire in an eyebolt to each, one at each end of the crossarm and one in the center. It is a good idea to twist one end of the wire to the first crossarm and to connect the other end of the wire to the second crossarm with a turnbuckle in order to keep the wire tightly stretched.

Training the kiwi vine to a trellis requires three seasons of pruning and tying. It takes this long for the trunk and lateral branches to reach their appointed places and mature. The goal of the first season is for the plant to grow into the overhead wires. This can be accomplished by tying the main stem of the vine to a 6- to 8-foot stake and by adjusting the stem occasionally to prevent it from twining around its support. Once the vine reaches the height of the wires, cut it back to 3 or 4 inches below the wires. As the vine grows, train two vines onto the wires in opposite directions. This will produce a sturdy Y-shaped trunk as the plant matures. As the plant continues to grow this first season, keep an eye on the ties so that they do not constrict the swelling branches. Trim any suckers that sprout from the main stem below the Y.

A kiwi's health, appearance, and fruit production depend partly on proper pruning. Both diligent, summer snipping of unproductive branches and suckers and dormant, winter pruning of spent vines are necessary. The basic rule for dormant pruning is to remove one third of the lateral branches each winter; start with those that show signs of illness or injury. Then thin those branches that have finished their second year of fruiting. Finally take out any branches that are twining around the wires.

If the plant's trunk has not yet reached the height of the wires in the first winter, cut it down to only four to eight buds, and resume training in the following spring.

The second summer will likely see that your efforts have been rewarded with a show of fruit. The side branches that form along the horizontal arms produce the fruit. Tie these side branches onto the outside wires of the trellis every 24 to 30 inches. Prune these canes 6 to 10 inches past the last flower bud (see illustration of flower bud on page 98). During the second winter, cut off all but two or three of the side branches that bore fruit, and shorten the main arms to about 5 feet long.

In the third summer, prune out any *late* sprouting side branches. They shade the fruit on other branches and do not bear fruit. The final step in training comes in the next winter when the two main lateral branches should be cut back to a length of 8 feet; these are the permanent base for the sprouting side branches. Each year allow enough side branches to grow to replace those that have finished fruiting. The branches will bear vigorously for two years, so new branches need to be encouraged every third year.

GROWING TIPS

A light feeding at planting time is beneficial, and two doses of a good, organic fertilizer each year thereafter are recommended. Feed early in the season before the vines begin to grow and then again after the fruit has set.

PESTS & DISEASES

These vines are among the most pest free and disease resistant you can grow. Birds are not usually a problem because the fruits do not ripen on the vine. If curious birds or critters do threaten the vines, spread netting over the trellis. Usually, absolutely no controls are necessary.

RIPE & READY

Test if the fruits are ripe by first letting some soften indoors for a few days before tasting. Kiwis will keep up to 6 weeks in the refrigerator when ripe and sweet, but will develop even more flavor if allowed to sit at room temperature for a few days.

The 1½-inch fruits are loaded with vitamin C and make excellent, healthful, bite-sized snacks. Remember, the skin is thin and edible. Try them pureed in fruit sorbet or as an unusual addition to fruit salads.

MELONS

Of the truly rare pleasures in life, sampling a freshly picked, vine ripened cantaloupe ranks among the most elusive. These temperamental treats are often bypassed by gardeners. But those uniform, often greenish, melons that are available in supermarkets are a far cry from what the resourceful gardener can produce at home. Although homegrown melons may be similar in appearance, that is decidedly where the comparisons end. Due to the demands of the market, mass-produced melons must be picked according to a schedule that is dictated by shipment and sales, not ripeness. Meanwhile, the home gardener strolls through his or her plot daily and inspects each fruit for those that have reached the peak of ripe perfection and picks one more perfect melon to enjoy with lunch.

The immense difference in the flavor and texture of homegrown versus supermarket melons is that once plucked from the vine, melons do not continue to ripen or sweeten. What you pick is what you get. Wouldn't you rather pick a melon that is scrumptious from your own backyard than a green gamble from the produce aisle?

VARIETIES

The other sad fact of market melons is the lack of variety. Although only a few different types are grown commercially, there are many varieties that are available for home growing.

Cantaloupes are a type of muskmelon. There are several, available varieties that differ in growth habit, days to maturity, and fruit. Some produce giant melons, some tiny. Cantaloupe skins turn from green to cream colored and form a raised netting as the fruit ripens. The flesh, however, may be bright orange, golden, salmon colored, or even green, when ripe.

Other melons that mature late in the growing season include Honeydew, Casaba, and Crenshaw. Honeydews typically have a pale green, lightly netted skin and firm, sweet, light green flesh. Intriguing varieties have been developed, however, that offer such unusual treats as amber-colored flesh and designer flavors, ranging from "tropical" to pear, apple, and pineapple. Casaba melons are round and come to a point at the stem end. The skin ripens to a golden yellow, while the flesh matures to a creamy white. Crenshaw melons can grow up to 14 pounds. The thick, salmon colored flesh is uniquely flavored. The skin turns to a greenish golden beige as the fruit ripens.

Still new to home gardeners are the "exotic" melons, such as Early Silver Line (Burpee). Originating in the Orient, these thin-skinned, oblong fruits offer yet more variety to the melon patch with crisp texture and rare, gourmet taste.

When it comes to melons, the granddaddy of them all is that all-time, summer favorite—the watermelon. There is quite a choice to be made for those who grow their own. Sizes range from little, 6- to 8-pound Sugar

Babies to enormous, 30-pound or more Charleston Grays.

Although most of us remember being banned to the outdoors to enjoy the sweet, bright red insides and to deal with all of those seeds by spitting for distance, there are a few surprises that are awaiting us all. Golden- and yellow-fleshed varieties, such as Tendersweet and Yellow Doll, have been developed; different flavors have been perfected, such as Hybrid Pineapple, at a diminutive 4 pounds. But by far the biggest thing to shake up the watermelon seed-spitting champs are the seedless varieties, such as Honey Red or Honey Yellow Seedless. The seedless hybrids offer not only a more polite eating experience, but also superior plant vigor, disease resistance, and incomparable texture and taste. Emily Post would be pleased.

SITE & SOIL REQUIREMENTS

Melons are sun worshippers. Give them a bright spot where no melons or other members of the cucurbit family (cucumbers, squash, pumpkins) have grown within the last three years.

They prefer a light, sandy loam with a pH level between 6 and 7.5. Good drainage is essential. In heavy soil, raised beds will enhance drainage. Adding organic matter also helps; soils rich in organic matter produce the finest melons. Compost or rotted manure that is added before planting time will get the seedlings off to a good start. Adding bonemeal, about ½ cup per foot of row, will help to promote early root growth. Cantaloupes are affected by boron deficient soils; add granite dust to compensate.

PLANTING

Melons are very tender plants and require 70 to 90 days of absolutely frost-free weather to reach maturity. In short season climates, this means starting the seeds indoors 2 to 4 weeks prior to transplanting.

Start 2 to 4 seeds in each peat pot, and later snip all but the very best. Keep the seeds moist and warm under lights or near a sunny window. When the soil is warm, set the seedlings into the ground in their peat pots (see page 44); this will help to prevent transplant shock. Be sure to completely bury the peat pots so that no part of the pot is showing.

Direct seeding can be done in hills, soil filled tires, or raised beds. Plant 4 to 8 seeds per hill, 2 to 3 inches apart and ½ inch deep. Hills should be spaced every 4 to 6 feet. If planting by rows, space the seeds every 6 to 12 inches in rows 6 feet apart. Thin to one plant every 12 to 18 inches. Most melons will germinate in 7 to 14 days. Watermelons should come up in about 10 days and will need more space than other varieties—one plant every 2 to 3 feet.

Seeds of the hybrid, seedless watermelons are somewhat different from other melon seeds and demand special treatment to germinate. They are covered with a sticky, wrinkled seed coat that hinders the seedlings as they try to break through. Start the seeds indoors; place each seed pointed end up in moist, seed starting mix. Keep them warm on a heating pad or cable, and as soon as the infant plants poke through, gently remove the constricting seed coat. Afterwards keep the young plants in a sunny window or under lights until transplant time.

TRELLISING

Yes, even these heavy-fruited vines can and should be trained up a trellis. A sloping support with a mesh at least 6 inches square is ideal. A 2x4 frame with wire mesh fencing or 1x2 wooden lattice as the plant support is perfect (see illustrations in Chapter 3).

Heavy melons will require a bit of trellis customizing; all but the smallest fruits should be supported by an individual sling (see illustration on page 17). Cheesecloth, discarded panty hose, plastic onion bag mesh, feed sack cloth, old sheets, or last year's bird netting can all be recycled. Cut the material to size for the melons that you are growing. Secure one end of the cloth to the trellis, and drape it underneath the developing fruit. Tie the other end of the cloth to the trellis to form a sling. Melons have also been grown well on a stout tepee by securing the slings to ropes that are wrapped around the trellis legs.

The trellis should be set up before the vines are 1 foot long. The vines will need to be guided to the support and then gently tied in place with soft cord or cloth.

GROWING TIPS

Melons prosper when they are mulched with plastic; it not only keeps weeds down and moisture up, but also helps to heat the soil.

Despite their large, juicy fruit, melons need only about 1 inch of water per week. They need extra water during very hot spells, but otherwise tolerate heat well. Water by drip or sunken container (see Cucumbers, page

45) to avoid the waste and possible disease spreading of overhead sprinkling. About two weeks before harvest, cut back the water. This tells the plant that it is time to stop enlarging the fruit and time to start concentrating sugar into it.

Both male and female flowers are present on each melon vine, and pollination depends on insects visiting both. If fruit fails to set, try hand pollinating (see Cucumbers, page 45). Seedless watermelons require pollination from an entirely different plant, so plant another variety nearby. Melons can cross-pollinate, but the results affect only the seeds.

Any flowers or fruit that form late in the season should be removed. They will not have time to ripen and will drain the plant of energy that is needed to mature those that set earlier.

Never use any products that contain sulfur on or near cantaloupes. A little compost or rotted manure, which is worked into the soil just as the vines begin to flower, will aid fruit set. Melon vines that have been stressed due to transplant shock, lack of water or nutrients, and pests or disease produce off tasting fruit or no fruit at all.

PESTS & DISEASES

Just about anything that bugs cucumbers will bug their relatives the melons (see Cucumbers, page 46). A tidy garden, crop covers, and regular, light cultivation will keep pests to a minimum. Pickle worms will chew right into the melons as will melon flies. Cover individual melons with a paper bag to protect them. Cucumber beetles may be discouraged by planting radishes, marigolds, and nasturtiums around the melon vines. Blast aphids off the undersides of leaves with water from the garden hose. Flea beetles only eat tender leaves, so cover transplants until the leaves outgrow the beetles' appetites.

Melons are susceptible to curly top, which is spread by leafhoppers. Fusarium wilt is spread by cucumber beetles. Prevent the spread of either disease by protecting the plants with crop covers. Just remember to remove the covers so that the plants can be pollinated.

There is no shortage of diseases that affect melons. Many are fungal and thrive in the warm, moist conditions that are supplied by sprawling vines. Trellising helps to keep diseases, such as anthracnose, powdery mildew, and leaf spot, from taking over. Mosaic is a serious, viral threat that causes symptoms from yellow, misshapen leaves to lack of fruit. It can be spread by contact, such as a meandering gardener or a splashing sprinkler. Honeydew melons tend to be the most resistant.

A major threat to watermelons in some areas are coyotes. They love nothing more than to take one big, sweet, dripping chunk from each melon on the vine—much harder to do when those fruits are elevated and cradled in a sling.

RIPE & READY

How do you tell when a melon is ripe? Do you sniff it, thump it, or look for telltale signs along those silent vines?

For cantaloupe, there is a simple test. By the time that the fruit has matured to a creamy color with a pronounced netting, you can begin to search for those perfectly ripe specimens. The stem will begin to crack in a circle at the point where it attaches to the melon. If it comes free with just a slight tug, the melon is ripe. Unfortunately, even overripe melons will pass this test.

The variety, Venus Hybrid Honeydew, will pass the "slip test"; Honeydew, Casaba, and Crenshaw melons will not. If you wait for the stem to slip free for these three melons, you will be waiting for it to rot off. Instead, once *these* melons reach a full ripe color, look for a slight softening at the blossom end, which is opposite from where the stem is attached, and gently pick the melon from the vine.

Watermelons have a list of harvesting tricks that is all their own. The last tendril of the leaf that is nearest the fruit turns brown and dries up; the skin becomes rough; if you thump it, there is a characteristic echo. Do not listen to your melons during the heat of the day because they all sound alike then. See what they have to say first thing in the morning. Once a watermelon has passed the point of just-right-ripe, it will still sound the same.

Cantaloupes are best served as fresh as possible at room temperature. Although they will keep for several days in the refrigerator, the flavor will deteriorate. They are great sliced, chunked, or scooped into balls for fruit salads. Gourmet melon sorbets and sherbets make great desserts.

Cantaloupes are rich in carotene, which converts into vitamin A. They also contain B vitamins, vitamin C, phosphorus, calcium, iron, and soluble fiber. Watermelons boast a wealth of vitamins A and C, as well as some iron and fiber. Melons do not store for long, so enjoy 'em while you got 'em.

PEAS

Oh, how gardeners need peas. They are the first to be planted in the garden in the spring. Their energetic growth, delightful, early flowers, and succulent, sweet pods all reward the gardener for getting an early start—the earlier the better.

VARIETIES

Peas may be divided according to growth habit or pod formation. While most pea vines reach for the sky, merrily scaling 6-foot trellises, some varieties stop short—with their dwarf vines reaching only about 30 inches tall. Different pod types are found in both of these categories.

Many varieties of garden peas vie for the gardener's attention in those very early, garden catalogues. Often the term "garden peas" applies to standard varieties, such as Maestro and Wando, or those that must be shelled. Snap peas are Sugar Snap, Sugar Daddy, Sugar Bon, or Sugarmel, which have sweet shells that can be eaten either whole or snapped. Snow peas are those wide, flat pods that are most familiar to nongardeners as a recognizable ingredient in Chinese take-out food. The pods of Oregon Sugar Pod II, Snowbird, Blizzard, and Mammoth Melting Sugar are sweet, tender, and delicious.

SITE & SOIL REQUIREMENTS

Although peas need full sun early in the season, partial shade during the summer is appreciated. Peas are cool season plants and will not flower or set fruit in very hot weather.

Peas do not require especially fertile ground. Like other legumes, they will improve the soil in which they grow by fixing nitrogen into it. A little compost or aged manure at planting time should supply all the nutrients that are needed for the plants to get a good start. Phosphorus or potash deficiencies can cause leaves to curl or turn purple. Wood ashes (5 to 10 pounds per 100 square feet) will provide both of these nutrients. Ashes also serve to buffer extremely acid soils. Peas do best in a pH range of 5.5 to 7.

Well-drained soil is essential to healthy pea vines. Plants take in oxygen through their roots, and soggy soil can deprive them of as much as 90 percent of the oxygen that they need. It also interferes with the plant's ability to take up nitrogen. Soils rich in organic matter are pea heaven not only because of the improved drainage, but also because of a healthy, nutrient content. Lighten clay soil by working in compost, peat, sand, or other organic matter. Try planting peas in raised beds. Not only do raised beds drain better, but also they reduce soil compaction around the plant roots, which is another cause of oxygen deprivation.

PLANTING

Peas do not take well to transplanting. There is nothing to be gained by starting these vines indoors. Direct seed, and get the earliest start possible with peas by preparing the planting site during the previous fall.

On the day before planting, soak the peas overnight in warm water to relax the tough seed coat. Soaking plumps up the dehydrated seed and helps to speed germination. It also makes them more receptive to inoculate (see Beans, page 35).

Plant the seeds 2 inches deep in heavy or warmed soil or 1 inch deep in lighter or still cool ground. Peas enjoy their own company and do well when they are crowded. Plant them in double rows, spaced 3 inches apart each way. Germination takes from 7 to 14 days in soil temperatures of 40°F or higher. Staggered plantings will yield over a prolonged season, as will plantings of early, midseason, and late ripening varieties. Plant a fall crop 60 to 70 days before the first expected, autumn frost.

TRELLISING

Pea vines are enthusiastic climbers that easily top heights of 6 feet or more. Grasping, coiling tendrils anchor the vines to any stationary support, including each other.

The type of trellis that is needed depends on whether standard or dwarf varieties are being grown. Even the shortest vines will flop into a tangled mass without some type of support. Branches that are pushed into the soil alongside the plants or 2-foot-tall pea fences will take care of the dwarfs, but the taller growing varieties need a more substantial support. A standard pea trellis must be tall enough to accommodate the length of the vines that will produce fruit all the way to their tops. Vertical fences of wire mesh fencing or either vertically or horizontally strung twine work well. Similarly fitted A frames are perfect for peas because two double rows can be grown side by side. Tepees are also good pea trellises. (See illustrations in Chapter 3.)

Until the vines find the plant support, they may need a little help. Lean the young vines into the support material, perhaps by weaving the tip of the vine between the strands. Once the tendrils contact the support, they will coil around tightly as the vine continues to grow upward. No other training is necessary.

GROWING TIPS

Peas are very hardy, vigorous, and fairly drought tolerant, but they cannot take the heat. Early planting is a must. The seeds must be kept moist to germinate, but once they sprout, they require surprisingly little water until they flower. At this point 1 inch of water per week will suffice. Drip irrigation is preferred for peas because it cuts wasted water and eliminates splashing. As with many other crops, this is a prime means of disease transmission. Also, remember to keep out of the pea patch when the vines are wet! Working among wet plants also spreads disease.

Thick mulch will keep the roots cool and moist and eliminate competing weeds. The roots and stems are fragile and easily damaged by cultivation or weeding.

PESTS & DISEASES

Birds will occasionally discover those tender, early pea sprouts. Netting, row covers, or a single wire that is strung over the rows should discourage them.

Hordes of pea aphids are among the vines' worst enemies; they suck juices and spread pea enation, a debilitating disease common in some areas. Pea weevils and disease-spreading thrips are a problem in other areas.

Many pea diseases can be avoided by choosing disease-resistant stock, practicing crop rotation, keeping weeds down, avoiding splashing water, and not working among wet vines. Fusarium wilt is a lethal, fungal disease to which several varieties, including Thomas Laxton and Green Arrow, are resistant. Bacterial blight, ascochyta blight, root rot, and powdery mildew are other pea problems. Among these problems, powdery mildew is the most common because it loves cool, damp weather as much as the peas love it.

RIPE & READY

Scrumptious peas! Sweet and crunchy in salads, mouth watering when lightly steamed with butter—they are a welcome addition to an early summer meal. Snow peas and sweet varieties, such as Sugar Snap, can be picked and enjoyed as soon as the pods form. Snap peas can be harvested anytime after the pods fill out. Do not wait too long, or the peas will begin to harden and lose their sweet flavor. Snap peas are at their peak when 2½ to 3 inches long and fat, but not lumpy.

Be careful not to damage the vines as you pick so they can continue to produce. A proper pea picker uses both hands. Hold the vine with one hand, and gently snap off the pods with the other. Like sweet corn, peas begin to convert sugar into starch soon after harvest, so be prepared to bring them to the table or the freezer as soon as they are picked and shelled. To shell, snap off the stem end and run a thumbnail down the seam of the pod to expose the peas. A smooth flick of the thumb back upward will pop them out. Work with your hands over a large bowl, and toss the hulls into a separate container. The empty pods are great for livestock.

Peas will keep in the refrigerator for over 1 week, but the flavor fails quickly. They are great for freezing, but most are not recommended for canning. They can also be dehydrated with good results. Fresh peas are rich in vitamins A, B_1, and C and contain vitamin K, phosphorus, and iron.

RASPBERRIES

What rare and precious rewards await the gardener in his or her very own raspberry patch. Delicately sweet/tart berries, heavenly when fresh picked, rapidly lose their form and flavor. A mere overnight stay in the refrigerator changes them from marvelous to mushy. The plants are terribly susceptible to viruses and sucker so readily that they often threaten to overrun the garden. Are such temperamental treasures really worth the trouble? You betcha!

VARIETIES

A raspberry is a raspberry if it pulls free of the core when picked. The white hull stays on the vine, while the delectable, tender fruit drops into your hand with barely a touch. There are many different varieties of several distinct types, but all have this in common. There are both trailing and freestanding types that yield either red, purple, black, or yellow berries. Harvests may come in the spring or with everbearing varieties, both in the spring and fall. In practice, however, everbearing varieties are usually allowed only to produce the fall crop.

Heritage is the standard to which all other varieties are ultimately compared. It produces medium-sized, firm, red fruits in July and September from stiff-caned, freestanding plants that excel almost anywhere. Indian Summer and September are other popular everbearing red varieties. Red varieties, such as Latham, Hilton, and Willamette, produce luscious, single crops in the late spring. Yellow varieties include Amber, a single crop raspberry and Fallgold, a double crop type. Cumberland and Blackhawk are black raspberries that bear a single, midseason crop. Purple varieties include the stiff-caned Brandywine, Royalty, and Amethyst.

In general, red varieties are considered to have the best flavor. Purple versions are credited with being juicier than black varieties, but the blacks have the best garden manners because they do not sucker. Reds require a good winter chill and do not do well in mild climates. Yellow berries are a striking contrast to anything else in the berry patch and are relished for their unusual color and fragrance. All raspberries are very hardy, and most require substantial winter chill to set fruit. Varieties especially developed to produce in warm climates include the red Southland and Dormared and the black Cumberland.

SITE & SOIL REQUIREMENTS

Red raspberries flourish wherever apple trees thrive, and black raspberries love peach country. This is probably due more to climate than to soil. A cold winter and a sunny summer is all that most varieties require. They will tolerate full sun in most areas, but if afforded some shelter from the hottest afternoon rays, they will do all the better. Berry patches that are situated along the east side of a building or fence fare very well.

Red raspberries like light, fertile soils; black varieties tend to favor deep, clay soils. All raspberries prefer a mellow, aged soil and demand good drainage. The plants also appreciate a high content of organic matter. A slightly acid to neutral pH level (6 to 7) is ideal.

PLANTING

In most areas, raspberries should be planted in early spring, but the job really begins in the previous fall. Prepare the bed 2 feet wide by 1 foot deep to whatever length you have designated as the raspberry patch. Once the soil is removed, you may want to line the trench with planks to prevent underground suckers from sneaking out. Shovel in a few inches of compost or manure, and refill with soil. Top with another layer of compost or manure about 6 inches deep. Mix the soil and amendments with a spading fork, and let the bed rest until spring when it will be in prime condition for planting.

Raspberry plants are available either mail order or through local nursery outlets. The advantage to buying locally is that you will most likely be offered varieties that have been proven in your area. Mail order, on the other hand, gives you a lot more choice and freedom to experiment. Your local nursery owner or extension agent can give you regional advice. Be sure to insist on plants that are certified virus free.

The plants will be shipped from early to midspring. Keep the roots moist until ready to plant, and, at that time, prune the canes to 9 or 10 inches above the crown. Set the canes in the ground so that the crown is at ground level, and the roots spread out evenly. Space the plants 18 inches apart, and leave about 5 feet between rows of red or gold varieties and 6 to 7 feet between rows of blacks or purples. Never plant red and black varieties together—experts recommend from 200 to 700 feet apart.

If you must prepare the soil in the spring, do this as early as possible to give the soil a chance to mellow; use only aged compost or manure. In most areas, red raspberries can be planted in the fall.

TRELLISING

Although stiff-caned raspberries are often sold under the claim that they need no trellising, they will only benefit from some guidance, and trailing varieties are doomed without it. Set up your trellis at planting time, and choose a design that suits both the berries and the site.

A fence-type trellis fits nicely into a narrow space or even against a wall (see illustrations on pages 22 and 23). Set heavy posts 8 to 10 feet apart and string with heavy gauge wire at two levels—one wire about 2 feet from the ground and the second wire 5 feet high. When the canes reach the wires, tie them in place and keep them thinned to 6 to 8 inches apart or a total of 7 or 8 per plant.

The very best design for raspberries is the V trellis, which was recently developed by plant scientists at Cornell University. It is very similar to a clothesline-type trellis, but the top wires are spaced farther apart than the bottom wires. The results are twofold: fruit laden canes can lean over the upper wires, while new shoots can rise in the open center to more sunlight and better aeration than in other trellis systems. Yield increases of up to 50 percent have been reported on converted test patches.

The V can be set up in at least two ways. The first way is similar to the clothesline trellis (see illustration on page 23), but instead of two crossarms, there are four. Set in sturdy posts every 20 feet and attach crossarms at two levels—one crossarm about 2½ feet up and a second crossarm about 5 feet high. Cut the top crossarm 3 feet long and the bottom crossarm 2 feet long. Fasten heavy gauge wires to each end of each crossarm, and pull tightly. Attaching one end of each wire to a turnbuckle will allow you to continue to control the wire tension.

Eight-foot steel fence posts can also be used. Drive the posts in about 2 feet deep in pairs that are set 1½ feet apart and angled away from each other at about 15° from vertical. The tops of the posts should spread about 3½ feet apart. Space the pairs of posts about 4 feet apart, and drive an anchor post at either end of the row. String one wire about 2½ feet from the ground and the other about 5 feet up.

V Trellis for Raspberries

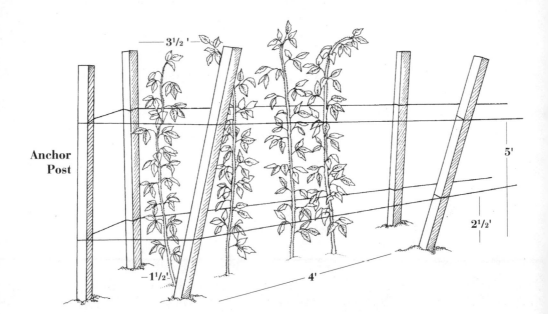

When training the vines, keep them thinned and tie the fruiting vines to the outside, which allows new shoots to come up in the middle. Cut the old canes out as soon as the harvest is in, and tie the newcomers in place.

GROWING TIPS

Like blackberries, raspberries are perennial plants that produce biennial vines. Standard varieties will bear fruit in their second or third season, and everbearing types will put out a small crop in their very first fall. The vines are treated differently depending on if they produce a single, summer crop or yield double harvests. Restricting everbearers to only a fall crop is the simplest method. Just mow them down with a lawn mower after they go dormant. In the following spring, little or no pruning will be necessary, and the plants will offer a big, juicy crop of berries early that fall.

Pruning the spring bearers is a little more involved. The biennial vines produce fruit in the second season when they are tied to a trellis. New shoots will come up during the summer as replacements for those vines that are currently in production. Keep these new shoots thinned as previously mentioned. As soon as the bearing vines are harvested, they should be cut out and destroyed to prevent diseases. At this time, the new canes can be tied in place. In the following spring, thin to the best canes per plant after removing any dead or winter damaged vines.

Do not top canes if they get too tall; the tips are the most productive parts of the vines. Pruning to encourage side shoots on fall bearers is another old practice that experts now discourage.

The raspberry patch will benefit from a top dressing of aged manure or compost every other year. Spread it around the base of dormant plants until spring pruning time. The plants require only ½ to 1 inch of water per week and seem to appreciate a thick, moisture-retaining mulch. Mulching helps to keep cultivation to a minimum and reduces the chances of sucker-prone roots. Late summer or early fall cultivation is also recommended because it helps to disrupt soil-dwelling pests.

Raspberry patches seem to decline every few years; most often this occurs because viral diseases get established. When this happens, it is time to relocate the patch. This can be done by allowing suckers to grow and digging them out or by tipping trailing varieties (see Blackberries, page 41). It is better, though, to start fresh with all new, certified, disease-free stock rather than to risk starting a new patch and find it infected. This also eliminates the risk of violating the patent on protected varieties, such as Redwing and Bababerry.

PESTS & DISEASES

For the host of pests and diseases that will attack raspberries, the best defense is cleanliness. Always remove and burn spent, diseased, or damaged canes, keep weeds down, and cultivate the soil to disrupt bug larvae and weed seeds.

Look out for spider mites, raspberry cane maggots, and raspberry fruit worms. Raspberry cane borers weaken canes and leave them open to disease. Some varieties are also susceptible to most blackberry pests. Most blackberry pests, however, do not bother raspberries because raspberries prefer a much cooler climate.

The biggest threat to raspberries are viral diseases; leaf curl, mosaic, and streak are among the most damaging. These three diseases are spread by aphids. Streak zeros in on black varieties specifically, while raspberry leaf curl strikes both black and red types. Orange rust and verticillium wilt affect black raspberries, while powdery mildew attacks all varieties. One disease that seems to prefer red varieties is spur blight. Other diseases that threaten raspberries include anthracnose, cane blight, and cane gall—all prefer the black varieties. All raspberries are subject to frost damage and winterkill.

RIPE & READY

While nothing compares with the sheer luxury of freshly picked raspberries topping a chilled glass of champagne, there are a few other notable ways to enjoy them. They make wonderful jams and preserves. The juice can be pressed for sublime syrups, cordials, liqueurs, or wine. Most varieties are satisfactory for freezing; Willamette is one of the most highly recommended.

Fresh raspberries are high in vitamin C and manganese and contain significant amounts of magnesium, zinc, potassium, niacin, and riboflavin.

SQUASH & GOURDS

Many gardeners draw the line right here. For those with limited space, the idea of these massive, trailing vines is disheartening. Although space saver, bush-type plants have been developed, squash are often still sacrificed because of the space that they still require. Do not make this mistake.

Squash are available in many amazing varieties of healthful, tasty fruits and are so prolific and easy to grow that no garden should be deprived of them. If space has been your only objection to the cornucopia of their various delights, or if plant diseases or poorly developed fruit have soured you on squash, cheer up! By trellising, you can grow beautiful, bountiful squash and gourds anywhere that you can spare a 3-foot circle.

VARIETIES

Squash and gourds offer some of the largest selections of plant varieties in the garden. They can be little, big, white, yellow, orange, and green with stripes and patterns galore. There are fancy scallops, bells, clubs, straight and crooked necks, and rounded shapes that are the size of tennis balls and beach balls. Squash are divided into summer squash and winter squash. Summer squash grow as squatty bushes and the winter varieties grow on endless, meandering vines.

Winter squash are harvested at maturity rather than at the more tender stages of development, such as with summer squash. One variety is the dark green, deeply ribbed Acorn, which includes such oddities as Cream of the Crop, a white-skinned version with the characteristic deep golden flesh, but with an unusual nutlike flavor. Butternut squash are another winter selection and grow into 2- to 3-pound yellow, bell shaped fruit with orangish flesh. Hubbard types include a range from "baby" to the outsized Blue Hubbard. The dieter's delight, Spaghetti Squash, with its pastalike flesh makes a great substitute for the real thing.

Pumpkins are also a type of winter squash. Teensy Jack-Be-Little grows to only 3 inches across, while massive Big Max and Atlantic Giant can squash the scales at well over 100 pounds. In 1989, an Atlantic Giant, weighing 755 pounds and measuring 12 feet in diameter, broke the previous world's record by 84 pounds! Show King is another monster that grows huge, white-skinned, pumpkin-like squash. Of course, to get pumpkins to reach these miraculous proportions requires special attention and the right variety.

Many pumpkin varieties are suitable either for their fine flavor or for jack-o'-lanterns, or both. Autumn Gold Hybrid, Jack O'Lantern, and Triple Treat are excellent all-purpose pumpkins; Small Sugar is treasured for its taste and texture.

Gourds offer even more variety in size, shape, and colorful patterns. Many are edible, especially when small, but most often it is their diverse usefulness that lands them a spot in the garden. Luffa gourds produce those expensive, natural "sponges." Bottle gourds form curvaceous fruits—perfect for bird houses or containers. Dipper gourds are made into ladles and other craft items. An assortment of colorful, dried gourds makes the Thanksgiving table centerpiece complete.

SITE & SOIL REQUIREMENTS

Like the majority of vine crops, winter squash and gourds grow best in full sun. They demand good drainage and plenty of water. Soil rich in humus will help to satisfy these requirements; work in compost or rotted manure to keep organic matter and nutrient levels high. Colloidal or rock phosphate can be added to boost phosphorus levels, and greensand or wood ashes can be supplied to raise the level of potash, if needed.

These plants prefer a slightly acid soil (6 to 6.5 pH).

PLANTING

Like all cucurbits, squash and gourds are extremely frost sensitive and choosy about transplanting, which can make getting an early start a frustrating experience. By catering to their needs, however, you can help them to adjust and flourish.

Start the seeds indoors in 4-inch peat pots no more than 4 to 6 weeks before the last frost. Once the garden soil is well warmed, transplant the seedlings to the garden in the pots, and make certain that the tops of the peat pots are well covered with soil (see page 44). Transplant in the evening or on an overcast day to diminish the shock, and transplant only after the tender plants have been well hardened off. Protect them at night for the first few weeks with covers, such as hotcaps or overturned buckets.

Like cucumbers and melons, squash and gourds benefit from raised beds or hill planting. They like the superior drainage and the warmer soil. Leave about 2 feet between plants in raised beds, or space hills so that the centers are about 4 feet apart. (Untrellised plants require much more space between them because the vines take up a lot of room.) Up to 4 transplants can go into each hill, or plant 8 seeds 1 inch deep, and snip out all but the best 3 or 4 as they grow. Mound the soil into hills about 18 inches across and 10 inches high, then form a depression in the center. The depression holds water and allows it to slowly drain to the plant roots rather than running off the sides of the hill. Seeds will not germinate in soil temperatures less than 60°F, so make sure the ground is warm before you plant.

TRELLISING

Squash, gourds, and all but the heaviest pumpkins can be easily trained up a trellis. Fruits from one to a few pounds will need no additional support. As the fruit gradually increases in size and weight, the vines grow ever stronger with the increasing burden. Some gardeners have grown 10 to 15 pounders without resorting to slings. Slings, however, are cheap insurance when it comes to a prize pumpkin or squash, so you may want to include them just to be safe (see illustration on page 17).

Several forms of trellises are suitable for squash or gourds. Tailor the design to fit your planting area and the type of fruit to be supported. Tepees of heavy poles, 8 feet long and at least 2 inches across, make a practical, sturdy, and inexpensive framework. Squash vines really appreciate the extra horizontal support that is provided by wrapping rope around the tepee legs. If planting in individual hills, a tepee trellis is perfect because it can be set up directly over the mound and can provide a leg to support each plant. Other designs that have proven successful with squash and gourds are fence types and V frames. (See illustrations in Chapter 3.) One inventive gardener enlisted three old, step ladders to stand guard over his squash hills with very satisfactory results.

You will need to have a few cloth strips available to occasionally tie the vines in place. For very large fruit, slings will not help much because the weight will tear them or pull down the vine support. The vines can still be trellised to good advantage, but those giant fruits will need a platform to rest on, such as one or two bales of straw.

GROWING TIPS

Squash and its relatives love a good soaking, especially in hot, dry weather. Drip irrigation is the preferred method because it cuts down on waste and disease-spreading splashing. A sunken container is a practical alternative for squash as well as for other vines (see Cucumbers, page 45). A thick mulch or plastic sheeting is very effective in retaining water. Veteran squash growers prefer plastic sheeting over conventional mulching materials, such as straw or grass clippings, because it not only keeps water in and weeds and bugs out, but also it heats the soil for those warmth-loving roots. Plastic sheeting can be rolled out over the length of the planting beds or cut to size and placed over each hill. (Cut an X over the center of each hill and fit the transplants through the plastic.) Be sure to weigh down the edges with a few shovelsful of soil or some heavy stones.

These vines require very little special attention. A little compost as they begin to set fruit will boost fruit bearing. Hand pollinating will guarantee fruit bearing if plants do not seem to be setting fruit themselves. Pick off flowers that form after midsummer since they will not have a chance to mature into fruit and will only drain the plant's energy if left in place.

There are a few tricks that can make growing squash and gourds especially fun. Gourds can be trained to take on unusual shapes as they grow. Tie twine around them, or place immature fruit into a bottle or mold, and watch them form. Customize future jack-o'-lanterns by cutting in eyebrows, a nose, or scars. These features will heal over into bumpy ridges as the pumpkin continues to develop.

For those king-sized pumpkins, old-timers used to concoct all kinds of outrageous tales of explanation. More likely the bizarre stories were a means of throwing off the competition. Try these steps to coax the most out of your pumpkin vines.

1. Start with a large growing variety, such as Big Max or Atlantic Giant.
2. At planting time, dig deeply to loosen the soil, and work in a full bushel of compost or rotted manure.
3. Plant 3 to 5 seeds or transplants, and thin to the strongest one in each planting.
4. For the first few weeks, pick off any blossoms that appear to make sure that the vine is well established when it does set fruit.
5. Hand pollinate to insure vigorous, well-shaped fruit that forms where you want it to form. Allow only 2 or 3 pumpkins to form per vine, and pinch off all other blossoms.
6. Once the fruits are the size of a grapefruit, choose your favorite, and cull the others—just one per vine.
7. Water daily, and supplement with weak manure tea every 10 days. Mulch thickly, or use plastic sheeting.
8. Support the pumpkin with a hay bale or other platform.
9. Encourage lots of vines and foliage since the leaves feed the growing giant, but keep all flowers pinched.
10. Protect from frost, weeds, and pests.

PESTS & DISEASES

Squash and gourds suffer from many of the same pests and diseases as their close relatives, cucumbers and melons. Good garden sanitation, elimination of nearby wild pest and disease hosts, such as milkweed, catnip, and wild cucumber, and trellising are vital to maintaining a healthy patch. Floating row covers are indispensable for pest protection for young plants and have the added benefit of retaining heat. If you pollinate by hand, you need only to remove the covers momentarily; otherwise, they must come off to allow nature to take its course.

The list of pests to watch for include aphids, cucumber beetles, pickle worms, squash bugs, squash vine borers, leafhoppers, corn earworms, and Mexican bean beetles. Watch for obvious damage, such as chewed leaves or tiny spots that are caused by feeding or the telltale tunnels and frass that are left by busy borers.

Cucumber beetles spread bacterial wilt, a serious threat to cucurbits; sick plants slowly wilt until they die. Test for this disease by cutting open the stem and squeezing out the juice. Stick your finger in the juice, and pull it away. If the juice sticks to your finger and pulls out in a string, the plant will soon die. Dig it up, and destroy it. In the future, try Acorn or Butternut varieties since they are the most disease resistant.

RIPE & READY

Harvest winter squash and pumpkins before the first, hard frost. Cut them from the vine, leaving a few inches of stem on the fruit. Let them cure for one or two weeks (at temperatures of 75° to 80°F, if possible) to harden the skin. Bring them in at night if temperatures threaten to dip below freezing.

Squash and pumpkins are root cellar favorites and keep very well at temperatures between 40° to 50°F for weeks or months. They can be canned or frozen in chunks or pureed to make delicious pies. They are wonderful steamed and served with butter and nutmeg or cubed for soups or stuffing. Both squash and pumpkins are high in fiber and vitamin A.

For a gourmet delicacy, try the squash flowers dipped in batter and deep fried or filled with meat, bread crumbs, or cheese stuffing. Save the pumpkin seeds and dry them; toast them with a little butter on a baking sheet for a super snack.

Spaghetti squash are ready to pick when they reach 8 to 10 inches long, weigh 3 to 6 pounds, and are yellow colored. Cure them for 1 week in a sunny spot, and store in a cool, dry place. Cook spaghetti squash by making two or three deep punctures in the skin. Boil whole for 30 minutes, or bake for 1 hour until the surface gives when it is pressed. Split the squash lengthwise, and discard the seeds. Remove and fluff the strands, and top with your favorite tomato sauce.

Luffa squash can be eaten like zucchini when the squash are small and tender, but are usually grown for their fibrous "sponges." They are very prolific plants. Harvest when they are fully mature; immature fruit will rot during the curing process. Size will vary, but the color of the squash should be straw colored when mature. Leave at least 1 inch of stem when cutting them from the vine.

If you have never tried to grow luffa squash, start with just one plant until you have experienced the work that is involved in preparing the sponges.

To make sponges, the fruit must be cured, skinned, cleaned, and dried; there are two methods. To cure, allow the squash to sit in a spot with good air circulation for about 1 week until thoroughly dry. Air cured luffas must be skinned and then soaked and worked to dislodge the remains of the flesh. Or soak the squash in water for 3 to 4 weeks. Soaking takes longer, but it separates the flesh and skin from the sponge, which eliminates much of the work. Be sure to change the soaking water every few days. The final step in either method is to completely dry the sponges and shake out the seeds. The sponges are useful for a variety of things—especially as a skin stimulant in the bath.

Gourds have been used traditionally as harvest time ornaments. Well cured, they will last for years to grace centerpieces, wreaths, and other craft projects, such as birdhouses and dippers. To help determine when to harvest, be aware that gourds weigh less at maturity than in the growing stages. When harvesting gourds, be careful not to bruise them, and do not harvest any that have been frostbitten; these are prime candidates for rot.

Cut gourds from the vine, leaving a few inches of stem on the fruit. Cure in a warm, dry, shady spot. Some varieties must be brought inside to finish curing since they can take months to thoroughly dry.

When cured, the shell will be tough and dry and can be carved, hollowed out, varnished, or waxed. For birdhouses, drill a hole about 1¼ inches in diameter in the side of the gourd and a small hole at the top and the bottom. Feed a wire through the top hole to hang the birdhouse; the bottom hole is for drainage. Paint or finish the birdhouse as you like, but the birds seem to prefer the natural look.

SWEET POTATOES

If climbing potatoes seem a little odd, you are probably accustomed to those plain, starchy Idaho spuds, not the moist, sweet tubers from the southland. Sweet potatoes, however, are members of the morning glory family, a clan well known for its climbing ability. Moreover, they are by no means restricted to the South, but can prosper well into the North. They have been grown successfully, often producing better yields in the nearly pest-free environment of northern plots, as far north as New York. Anyplace with 100 frost-free days can relish the sweet rewards of these generous vines.

Sweet potato vines grow thick, lush, and long. Allowed to sprawl, they can form a solid mat of stems and foliage. This may have its advantages, such as choking out weeds and maintaining soil moisture, but it also has some downfalls. Trellising those ranging vines lets you enjoy all the benefits, as well as beat all the problems, such as the remarkable amount of space that sweet potatoes can consume at ground level, the tangled harvesting conditions of the evergrowing storage roots, and the habit of stems to send out new roots wherever they touch the ground.

VARIETIES

Much progress has been made in the development of pest- and disease-resistant, sweet potato varieties. Southern Delight and Excel are reported to have more natural insect resistance. They also boast wonderful flavor and high yields.

The standard varieties for comparison are Jewel, which adapts well to a variety of climates, produces well, and stores for nearly a year, and Centennial, an old favorite. Both send out long vines that are perfect for trellising. Even shorter stemmed varieties, such as Porto Rico, Gold Rush, and Vardaman, grow vines up to 5 feet long.

The most popular sweet potato varieties have long been those of moist, deep-colored flesh—often miscalled yams. Botanically, sweet potatoes are not remotely related to true yams, but a distinction is made between this orange-fleshed favorite and the drier, light yellow-fleshed varieties of sweet potatoes, such as Nuggett. Cultivars also have been developed in other colors: Regal is a purplish, red-skinned sweet potato that is nutritious, tasty, and insect and disease resistant; Sumor and White Delight are nearly white fleshed; Rose Centennial has rose-colored flesh.

Early producing varieties are recommended for short season growing. Some varieties to try are Carver, Georgia Jet, and Travis. Caromex is a variety that is suited to desertlike areas, and Pope was created for areas that are prone to flooding.

SITE & SOIL REQUIREMENTS

Sweet potatoes are an easy crop, especially in areas with lots of sunshine. They are very drought tolerant and love the sun.

If possible, prepare the soil bed early, and give it time to mellow before transplanting sweet potatoes. They prefer light, sandy, well-worked soil. Their roots can grow as deep as 8 feet, but they will produce nicely in porous soil that is well worked to a depth of only 8 inches. They have a fairly high demand for phosphorus and potash and will fail to produce in soils with too much nitrogen; the plant sends out all vines and few, if any, storage roots in nitrogen-rich soil. A somewhat acid soil from 5.5 to 6.6 suits them best.

PLANTING

Sweet potato plants grow from slips that form on the roots. You can order these through the mail or occasionally find them in a garden center, but they are easy to start at home. Use only the best roots to propagate seedlings because you want to pass along only the best traits to next year's crop. Be sure the roots that are selected for propagation came from plants that produced well—6 uniform potatoes per plant is a respectable yield.

Start slips indoors 6 to 8 weeks before the last expected frost. One method is to set the root (sweet potato) in a shallow container with the narrow end of the root tilted up; this is called the proximal end, which means the end that grew closest to the plant. The other, or distal end, will not normally send up shoots, but will sprout roots. Cover the root 1 inch deep with light, moist, potting soil and set in a warm place. Keep it quite warm, about 80°F, or the potato will not sprout. Placing the container on a heating pad or coil will regulate the temperature.

Cut slips from the root when they are about 8 to 10 inches tall and have at least 6 swollen leaf nodes. Do not be concerned about the slip's roots; a healthy slip quickly will send out new roots. Be sure the soil is warm, about 70°F, and that the last frost is well behind you before setting out the slips.

Another method for starting slips is to cut the end from a growing vine and root it in potting soil. Nurture the vine tip over the winter, and cut and root more slips from it. By late the next spring you can have many well-started sweet potato plants to set out.

The best method for planting sweet potatoes is to lay them down horizontally at a slight angle so that only the tips show above the ground. The underground nodes send out more roots, and the plants are more likely to survive and produce greater quantities of evenly sized potatoes than those that are planted vertically. Space the slips 12 to 15 inches apart and water well. They are guaranteed to wilt soon after planting, but most spring back within 3 days.

TRELLISING

Even though the trellis will hold only the vine and not the crop, it still must bear considerable weight. Sweet potato vines grow long and leafy and resemble a large-leafed ivy. They make attractive screens and can be situated so that the vines can serve that purpose, while the roots are serving another. A fence-type trellis with heavy wire mesh or an A frame or tepee with extra rope supports work well (see illustrations in Chapter 3). Train the vines into the supports by weaving them in and out of the mesh or ropes. Tying may help, but is usually not necessary.

One advantage of trellising sweet potatoes is that the vines can no longer root at will. This prevents them from establishing new batches of tiny, sweet potatoes that sap strength from the plant and result in lots of little sweets along the stems and few, if any, good-sized spuds.

GROWING TIPS

Roots begin to swell in the first 6 weeks. This is the most important time to keep weed competition down. Mulching is not widely recommended for preventing weeds because it cools the soil; only those gardeners in very warm areas can use mulch on sweet potatoes. Northern gardeners may try using black plastic mulch since it helps to heat the soil. Raised beds are recommended not only for their superior heat retention, but also because they spare the plants from soil compaction around the swelling roots. The plants need about 1 inch of water per week.

Trellising greatly limits the plant's ability to send out rootlets. Strip any side shoots that sprout along the first 10 inches of each vine to make sure that there are no ground level contact points.

PESTS & DISEASES

Sweet potato weevils are the worst threat to sweet potato growers. The good news is they do not bother northern gardeners. Sweet potatoes are also susceptible to root knot nematodes that can destroy the harvest by feeding on the roots.

Several kinds of rot can affect sweet potatoes in the ground and in storage. Black rot, soft rot, and stem rot can be slowed by practicing crop rotation and can be avoided by starting with disease-free slips. Scurf is another fungal disease that can be bypassed by planting healthy slips in ground that has not been planted in sweet potatoes within the last three years.

The best insurance against disease is to start with healthy slips. Cut new slips from the stem at least 1 inch above the soil line, and propagate as previously described for pest- and disease-free plants.

RIPE & READY

Sweet potatoes continue to grow as long as they are in the ground. They can reach impressive sizes, but those of average proportions are generally the most popular.

To harvest, begin digging before the soil temperature falls below 55°F. This temperature is important enough to buy a soil thermometer and to begin monitoring the soil a few weeks before the first suspected frost. Sweet potatoes are very tender, and those that are nipped by frost loose flavor and rot resistance. It is much better to dig a little too soon than a little too late.

Dig from the outside of the bed toward the plant, and be careful not to scratch, bruise, or damage the roots. Do not let the sweet potatoes sit out in the sun for more than a few minutes, while you are harvesting, or they will suffer sunscald.

To keep in storage, sweet potatoes must be properly cured. A week of 85° to 90°F and 80 to 90 percent humidity will thicken their thin skins and seal any wounds that might otherwise provide an entry point for rot. They can be cured outdoors if constantly shaded or in a cold frame, attic, outbuilding, or other protected place where you can control, or at least predict, the temperature and humidity.

Cured sweet potatoes call for somewhat unusual storage conditions. A temperature of 55° to 60°F, warmer than the root cellar but cooler than room temperature, and 80 to 90 percent humidity will keep them best. Do not let them freeze even for a little while; this transforms them into hard, inedible lumps. Sweet potatoes are rich in carotene, vitamin C, and fiber.

TOMATOES

Until the middle of the last century, tomatoes were believed to be as deadly as their close relatives, henbane and belladonna. To indulge in the succulent, red flesh was to flirt with death. Surely only fools or witches would dare the tempting fruit. Natives of the Americas, however, had long enjoyed the refreshing taste of tomatoes and after overcoming the skepticism and sometimes outright dread of suspicious settlers, soon found themselves sharing the bounty of their ruddy harvests. Today the tomato stands out as the king of home garden vegetables—the single, most popular plant grown.

VARIETIES

If plant breeders were to select a pet, the tomato would likely be it. There must be immense satisfaction in working with such a popular plant, especially one that has so many intriguing qualities with which to experiment. Hundreds of tomato cultivars exist today. They are either true breeding or hybrids, indeterminate or determinate, early, midseason, or late fruiting with cherry, small, midsized, large, or jumbo fruit of pink, red, orange, yellow, white, or green in either round or pear shapes. Some are hollow, some thick and meaty. Some have inbred resistance to diseases and pests. There are even notable differences in nutritive values.

True breeding or open-pollinated varieties are those from which the seed can be saved to produce plants much like those of the parents. All the old-fashioned varieties are true breeding. Hybrids are the product of two different strains that are bred together. Hybrids are more vigorous and hardy than the true breeding, but their seed is either sterile or produces unpredictable, inferior offspring.

The distinction between indeterminate and determinate tomatoes is one of growth habit. Indeterminate tomatoes continue to grow, flower, and fruit until killed by frost. The vines can become extremely long. They usually ripen large fruit late in the season. Determinate varieties grow until they reach their genetically determined limit, regardless of the best conditions. The vine ends in a cluster of flowers and will grow no further. These generally produce early, smaller fruit.

Early fruited or short season varieties are popular with northern gardeners or with anyone who wants to get a jump on the season. Varieties such as Siberian, Santiam, or Sub Artic are credited with producing mature fruit in as little as 45 days from transplanting. Some late season varieties have been developed for heat tolerance to carry them through long, hot summers; Hotset and Porter are good examples.

Differences in size have also been exploited by tomato breeders. Cherry tomatoes dangle in grapelike clusters either from indeterminate vines, such as Sweet 100 or Red Cherry or from determinate or dwarf plants, such as Tiny Tim or Red Robin. Beefsteak and Big Boy are prized as large, slicing tomatoes that yield fruits of 1 pound or heavier. The world's largest tomato was a scale-tipping, 7-pound 2-ounce Delicious.

Although bright red Better Boy or Whopper tomatoes make the mouth water with anticipation, they are only the beginning of the rainbow. Pink Girl produces fruits with a delicate blush. Sundrop tomatoes are deep orange, while Jubilee is a burnished gold and Lemon Boy and Gold Nugget are bright yellow. There is also a startling ivory variety called White Beauty. While most are round, Yellow Pear offers not only a tomato of a different color, but also produces an unusual, small, perfectly pear shaped tomato.

Some differences in the fruit, however, are not as obvious as size, color, or shape. Liberty Bell is hollow and perfect for stuffing, while Nova, Roma, and San Marzano are known as paste tomatoes for their thick, meaty flesh. Carogold and other orange-colored varieties derive their color from exceptionally high levels of carotene, and Doublerich contains higher than normal levels of vitamin C. Long Keeper takes several months to ripen once picked and will store most of the winter at room temperature.

Although not outwardly evident, the most important advances in tomato breeding are those of disease resistance. The devastating effects of many common tomato diseases can be easily avoided simply by planting disease-resistant varieties. Celebrity Hybrid is noted for strong plants that are resistant to fusarium wilts (I and II), verticillium wilt, tobacco mosaic virus, and nematodes. Disease resistance in plants is of such extreme importance that it is usually noted by abbreviation in the names of such varieties. Look for names such as Hybrid Gurney Girl VFNT.

No matter what the color, shape, or season in which a tomato ripens, the bottom line is taste. As you scan those brilliantly illustrated pages of seed catalogues, note what is mentioned first under each entry. If the color, size, growth habit, shape, earliness, or disease resistance is the most notable aspect of any given variety, that is what the catalogue will put first. But if the flavor is outstanding, they will say so right up front.

SITE & SOIL REQUIREMENTS

Tomatoes ask for only the best. Lots of sunshine and a well-drained soil that is rich in organic matter and well-balanced nutrients will keep them happy. They prefer a fairly acid soil with a pH from 5.5 to 6.5. Be sure not to plant tomatoes or related crops, such as peppers or eggplant, in the same area more than once every three years.

Too much nitrogen in the soil produces lots of vine and little fruit. A little bonemeal or colloidal phosphate when added to the soil at planting time not only helps to balance a high nitrogen content, but also helps to produce strong, healthy plants. Deficiencies or excesses of any essential nutrient in the soil show up in tomato plants in characteristic symptoms that make these plants prime indicators of soil condition.

PLANTING

Although most gardeners instinctively know that tomatoes have to be transplanted, tomatoes can also be sown directly into the garden. The benefits of direct seeding include bypassing all of those steps of transplanting, providing heat and light, and hardening off the seedlings.

Directly seeded tomatoes grow stronger from the start than their coddled counterparts and soon grow to equal the transplants or even surpass them. Plant the seeds in mid to late April. Space groups of 3 to 4 seeds about 2 feet apart, and cover with ¼-inch sifted soil. Water thoroughly with a fine mist, and keep moist.

Although seeds usually germinate in 7 to 14 days, cool soil will slow their emergence. You can speed things up a bit by prewarming the soil by laying plastic sheeting over the prepared seedbed for 2 weeks prior to planting. Keep the seedlings covered as they sprout and grow to protect them from frosts. After the third set of leaves appears, snip off all but the best plant in each group. Some varieties are better suited to direct seeding. You may have to experiment to see which ones do best for you. Beefmaster VFN, Roma VF, Ultra Boy VFN, and Ultra Girl VFN have all been successfully grown from direct seeding.

To start your own tomato transplants indoors, sow seed ¼ inch deep in a container that is filled with 3 inches of a good seed-starting mix. Get a head start by presprouting seeds before placing them in the growing medium (see Beans, page 35). If kept warm, the seeds should sprout in about 1 week. Provide bottom heat with a heating coil to encourage root development.

Tomato seedlings have two basic needs that must be met as soon as they sprout. Strong, even lighting will help them grow stout and green. Hang florescent lights within 4 inches of the tops of the plants, or keep them on a table by a sunny window and turn them occasionally to prevent lopsided growth. The seedlings also need room to grow healthy roots. Unlike many transplants, tomatoes thrive when repotted. The secret is to graduate to increasingly deeper containers for each repotting. After removing all but the top few leaves, set the seedling deeper into the new soil than it grew previously (only the top leaves should show), and the stem will send out more roots along the buried portion. The extra roots help to produce stronger, stockier, more vigorous seedlings than those grown in their original containers. The soil must be kept moist, and temperatures should dip no lower than 50°F for the best growth. Common problems with plants that are started indoors are too warm temperatures and insufficient light, which together produce tall, spindly, pale plants.

Before setting out transplants, be sure to harden them off. This is the physical process that toughens the plants to outdoor conditions, such as direct sunlight, wind, and temperature fluctuations, by gradually strengthening the cuticle, or outer layer, of its stems and foliage. Begin by setting the potted plants outdoors in a protected place for a few hours a day, and then gradually lengthen the duration as you increase exposure to the elements.

After about 1 week of adjustment, your tender seedlings should be tough enough to survive in the garden. Be prepared to protect them at night with hotcaps, plastic milk jugs (cut off the bottoms), or a plastic cover. The Wall O' Water is a great invention that uses water as insulation between two layers of clear plastic. The water warms during the day and releases its warmth to the plants at night (see Appendix II).

Transplant in the evening or on an overcast day to reduce stress on the plants. Prepare the soil, and dig holes deep enough so that you can set the young tomato plants in deeper than they were growing in their containers. Prune all but the top few sets of leaves, and bury the plant to within 2 or 3 inches of the top. Besides forcing new roots, this also reduces moisture loss through the leaves, a common cause of transplant stress and failure. Water well, and keep evenly moist.

TRELLISING

There are nearly as many means of training tomatoes as there are gardeners who grow them. Most methods require tying because tomatoes do not climb; they support their weight by leaning against whatever is available.

One traditional method is to drive a sturdy stake about 2 inches thick and 6 to 8 feet long into the ground at the base of the plant. As the tomato vine grows, it is periodically tied to the stake and pruned to maintain its form. Pruning consists of removing the suckers that grow in the joints between the main stem and a lateral branch. If left in place, these soon rival the trunk of the plant in size. Determinate tomatoes, however, should *not* be pruned because removing any of their branches will reduce the yield.

Cages are the second most common way of containing rangy tomato plants and the most appropriate method for determinate varieties. The ready-made tomato cages are almost always disappointing because they just are not big enough. You can easily make your own by using tomato cage wire, field fencing wire, or any suitable wire mesh with at least 6-inch openings in the mesh.

The simplest cages to make are cylinders. Bend the wire into shape and secure with clips, or twist pieces of wire around contact points to hold the cylindrical shape. Square cages can be made by cutting panels from wire mesh and clipping or wiring them together at the corners. All cages should be tied to stakes to prevent them from being blown over (see illustrations on pages 24 and 25).

Attractive cages can be made from 1x2 lumber. Use 6-foot wooden posts for the corners, and nail or screw 1x2s to form ladders across the middle and top of the cage. Set the cages in place and shove the posts into the soil to anchor the cages.

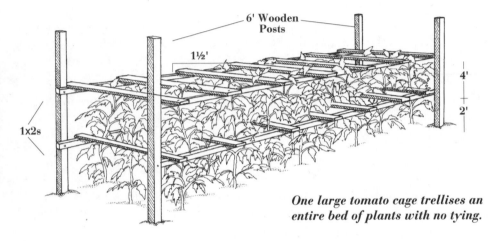

One large tomato cage trellises an entire bed of plants with no tying.

A wire mesh arch is even easier than a cage. Cut a 6-foot section of wire mesh, and bend it over the young tomato plant to form a tunnel. Draw the stems through the mesh as the plant grows, and allow them to amble down the sides (see illustration on page 25). No tying or other training is necessary.

Tomatoes can also be trained to a variety of fences. A good, simple fence consists of 4- to 6-foot wooden stakes or posts driven between the plants with (Number 9) wire or twine that is woven between the stakes on either side of the plants. The plants lean on the wires or twine and need no tying. Arrange the rows to run north and south, and drive the stakes into the ground at a 20° to 30° angle toward the west. The weight of the fruit causes them to hang from the underside of the fence on the west side. Consequently, the morning sun hits the base and sides of the plant, while only the tops get full sunlight during the heat of the day. The fruit is protected from too much sun by the overhead canopy of leaves. An A frame trellis and a

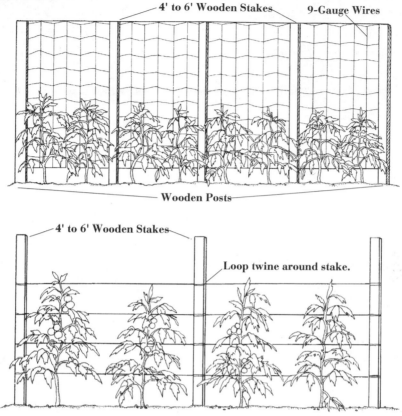

running tepee trellis work in much the same way (see illustrations in Chapter 3).

Another inventive fence is a zigzag fence (see illustration on page 90). Cut 2½-foot panels from 4-foot-high wire mesh so that one side is smooth and the other side has wire ends sticking out. Bend these ends over the smooth end of the next panel to form a hingelike connection. Set the fence up over a row of tomato plants in a zigzag so that each plant is supported on two sides. The open end makes the plant accessible for pruning, weeding, tying, and harvesting. Be sure to anchor the fence at the ends and the center with 6-foot metal or wooden stakes that are driven 2 feet into the ground. One of the best things about this fence is that after the harvest is over and the vines are cut away, it quickly and neatly folds for storage.

It is a good idea to set a tomato trellis up as soon as the plants go into the ground to avoid damaging the roots. This is especially true with designs

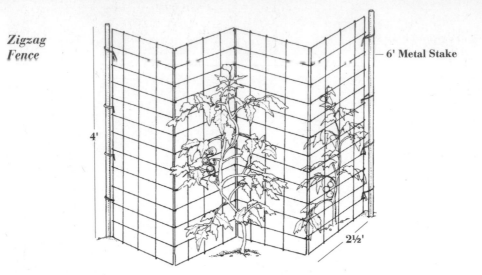

Zigzag
Fence

— 6' Metal Stake

4'

2½'

that require a post or anchoring stake that must be driven into the ground. An added benefit to putting the framework up early is that the frame can be used for cold protection simply by draping plastic sheeting or an old blanket over the top whenever cold weather threatens.

GROWING TIPS

Try arranging trained tomatoes around the base of a compost pile for healthy, carefree plants. Or, you may want to give them a few feedings over the season with fish emulsion. You can work compost into the soil near the roots anytime after the tomatoes begin to flower.

Erratic watering wreaks havoc on tomatoes. A dry spell that is followed by a soaking causes the fruit to crack and leaves them vulnerable to decay. Keep plants evenly moist to prevent any sudden shifts in the available water supply as the plants grow. About the second week in August, stop watering. As the soil dries out, the plants are stressed and soon come to realize that the end is near, which causes them to focus their energies into ripening their species' perpetuating fruit.

Trick heavily bearing, determinate varieties into producing earlier, larger, and tastier fruit by removing from half to two-thirds of the flowers. Always pinch off late forming flowers so that the plants will concentrate on ripening the fruit that has already set.

Tomatoes are tender, but adequate frost protection can make all the difference between a long, productive season or skimpy plants with a few green tomatoes. Young plants can be transplanted in the ground much earlier if covered with a cloche, Wall O' Water, or other suitable device. Loaded vines have a much better chance of yielding vine ripened fruit if you are ready with some blankets on that first freezing night. Often a cold snap is followed by days or even weeks of fruit-ripening, sunny weather. Be prepared.

PESTS & DISEASES

Tomatoes are susceptible to a dismaying multitude of maladies. From environmental problems and nutrient deficiencies to animals, bugs, and fungal, bacterial, and viral disease organisms, the tomato patch seems constantly under siege.

The best way to protect your tomato crop is through good garden management. Some things you cannot control, such as temperature. Temperatures below 50°F slow plant growth and hinder fruit set. The same thing happens when daytime temperatures rise to 90°F or nighttime lows exceed 70°F. Too much sun will scald the fruit; uneven water will crack it. Blossoms may drop from any type of stress, which costs fruit production. Catfacing, or unevenly developed fruit, results from uneven pollination. The best that you can do to help your plants is to cover the plants during cold spells, shade them from too much sun, water evenly, and prevent as much stress as possible. Tomato plants are also very sensitive to soil imbalances; these may be avoided by incorporating compost or rotted manures that are rich in nitrogen, phosphorus, and potash, and secondary and trace minerals into the soil.

Garden management also means keeping weeds and pests down and scouting for any early warning signs of disease. Often by pulling one sickly plant, you can spare the rest of the patch. Weeds not only compete for water, nutrients, and sunlight, but also harbor pests and diseases. And pests, not content with the damage they inflict while feeding, are also vectors for disease.

Bugs galore wait to attack tomato seedlings. Nematodes damage roots and spread disease; select the varieties of tomatoes that are resistant. Aphids, flea beetles, Colorado potato beetles, psyllid nymphs, whiteflies, and hornworms gnaw the foliage. Cutworms make short work of tender stems, and stalk borers hollow out mature stems. Stink bugs and tomato fruit worms ruin the fruits as they ripen.

The list of debilitating diseases is no less disarming. Some of the worst diseases, verticillium wilt, fusarium wilt, and tobacco mosaic, can be sidelined by growing resistant varieties. Others, such as anthracnose, blight, septoria leaf spot, and buckeye rot can be prevented by starting with clean seed in soil that has not been planted in tomatoes or related plants, such as peppers or eggplant, within the last 2 or 3 years. Water by drip irrigation to prevent spreading disease, and do not work among the plants when they are wet. If all else fails, pull out any suspicious looking plants.

Bacterial and viral diseases are best fought the same way. Bacterial canker and bacterial wilt are seed and soilborne, respectively. Viral diseases are often spread by insects or incubated in nearby weeds. Curly top may come to your tomato patch via leafhoppers, while mosaic viruses commonly inhabit wild plants and flowers. Such diseases make weed and pest control a top priority.

RIPE & READY

Next to a vine ripened tomato, those round, vaguely red-colored, supermarket versions might as well be waxed fruit. Except for Long Keeper, which was developed to ripen in storage, leave tomatoes on the vine until fully ripe. Red varieties are at their peak about 5 to 6 days after attaining their full color. Look for deep, true pinks, oranges, golds, or yellows to develop in other colored varieties, and then wait a few days to harvest. Do not let any tomatoes get nipped by frost; this affects flavor and storage. Be ready with those blankets if an early frost threatens, or pick all the tomatoes from the vines and bring them inside. Those with a hint of color will ripen in a few days at room temperature or in a few weeks in the root cellar. Green tomatoes can be used in special recipes (see *Tomatoes! 365 Healthy Recipes for Year-Round Enjoyment*, Garden Way Publishing, 1991).

When picking tomatoes, pull gently to free the fruit from the vine. Take care not to bruise the fruit or damage a vine that is still ripening other fruit.

Different types of tomatoes are suited to different uses. Paste tomatoes are best for sauces. Most tomatoes can be canned; a pressure canner is recommended for those with low acid content. Never can overripe tomatoes in a water bath because the acidity of tomatoes begins to decline as soon as they start to ripen. Tomatoes can be dried, and the slices can be used in cooked recipes. Dried slices can be pulverized in a food processor and used in powdered form. But the best use, while in season, is to eat tomatoes fresh from the vine. This is when their vitamin content, including vitamins A, C, and K, is at its peak.

ESPALIERED FRUIT TREES

No ancient art more successfully marries the best of form and function than does espalier. The training of fruit trees or ornamental trees and vines to conform to a trellis dates back to Roman times. The word *espalier* is a French derivative of the Italian word *spalliera*, which means something to lean or rest the spall (shoulder) on. In short, it is the practice of training trees to grow in patterns along a single, flat plane. This is accomplished by tying, propping, and pruning according to the desired outcome. It results in living and growing works of art and bountiful, mouth-watering harvests. Espalier is a wonderful way to satisfy your hunger for beauty as well as for delicious fruit.

No garden need go without the sweet scent and elegant beauty of flowering fruit trees or the rich rewards of their harvest. By training fruit trees to conform to a trellis, you can enjoy abundant yields of full-sized fruit from "pint-sized" trees. Even the most limited garden can spare room for one or two espaliered fruit trees since they occupy only a few inches of ground space.

Although the trees are lovely and make an interesting landscaping statement, these are not the best reasons for training them. Espaliered fruit trees enjoy all the same benefits as other trellised crops. Although many adventurous gardeners undertake espalier for the elegance and prestige that the trees may bestow upon their gardens, once the trees are established and producing, such lofty notions give way to the surprising realizations that it is not that difficult to practice espalier, and it is very enjoyable and practical.

ESPALIER DESIGNS

The shape of an espaliered tree may be formal or informal. Formal designs require more exact training and pruning over a period of years, but an informal design also demands its share of attention. The main difference is that the gardener follows a preconceived pattern in formal espalier, while informal espalier allows nature more of a hand in the design. Informal espalier still requires adequate shaping to maintain the two dimensional effect and sufficient pruning to promote productivity.

Shaping and exact pruning set espaliered fruit trees apart from all other fruit trees, and both gardening practices serve specific purposes. Shaping causes the tree to grow into the desired form. It enables trees to be trained into tight spaces, against walls, into hedges, or in an endless array of eye-appealing designs. Pruning facilitates shaping and increases aeration and ventilation, which helps to keep the tree healthy by minimizing humid, stagnant air pockets that are sought by disease organisms. It removes nonfruiting wood and promotes vigorous growth and fruit production. Diseased or damaged wood is pruned to maintain the overall health of the tree.

Formal Espalier. Trees may be trained to grow in an unlimited variety of shapes and designs depending on the artistic expression of the creative gardener. Many patterns have become established as traditional because of their elegant appeal and their practicality.

The simplest example of an espaliered tree is one trained in a single arm, or cordon (see page 95). It may be trained vertically, at an angle (oblique), or horizontally from the tree trunk. A row of such trees becomes a living fence.

Two horizontal cordons trained in opposite directions creates a T-shaped tree. This can be expanded to create a T in as many levels as desired (see page 95). These are easy to train and are well suited to apples and pears.

Two vertical cordons may be trained from a horizontal base to form a U shape, which can be further expanded into double or triple U's. The cordons may also be trained into a V, a shape that lends itself to a number of variations. Several V's planted in a row will crisscross to form a Belgian Fence, which if allowed to grow one or more side arms in a 45° angle creates a Losange. Both are beautiful patterns and are useful as screens and for fruit production. The V's may also be continued upward into a Palmette Oblique pattern, a single vertical trunk with V's centered along the middle; a Palmette Verrier, a variation of the Palmette Oblique in which the cordons are trained vertically into a candelabra shape; a Gridiron pattern,

Formal Espalier Patterns

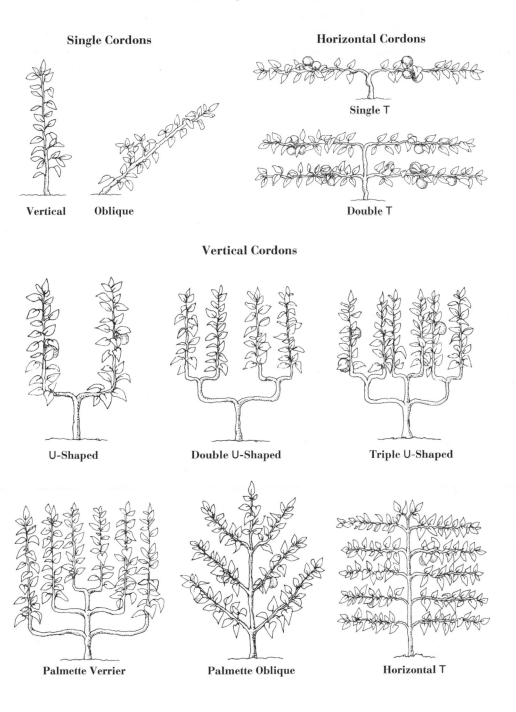

Single Cordons

Vertical   Oblique

Horizontal Cordons

Single T

Double T

Vertical Cordons

U-Shaped   Double U-Shaped   Triple U-Shaped

Palmette Verrier   Palmette Oblique   Horizontal T

a variation of the Palmette Verrier in which the horizontal cordons are also trained vertically (see all of these illustrations on pages 95 and 96).

An Arcure espalier produces an interlocking screen. The pattern at maturity forms arches upon arches. It is created by bending a single cordon into an arch and by allowing only one bud to develop from the top of the arch that is growing in the opposite direction from the original arch. Conveniently, the downward bending causes the branch to stop growing.

Informal espalier. The Fan variation is considered a more informal design in which several cordons arise from a low trunk at different angles.

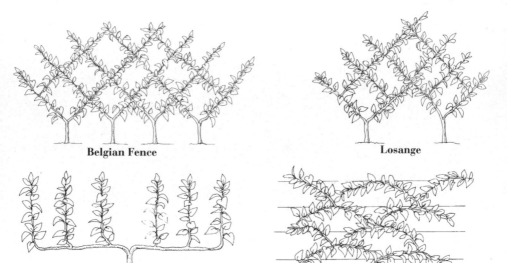

Belgian Fence **Losange**

Gridiron **Arcure**

Informal Espalier Patterns

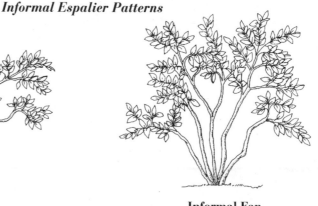

Free-Form Fan **Informal Fan**

PLANTING

Dwarf fruit trees are best suited to espalier because they have been bred to occupy a small space. Like other fruit trees, most dwarfs are actually two trees in one—an upper fruit-producing variety that is grafted to a dwarfing rootstock. Be particular about the rootstock that you choose because this has more influence on the size of the mature tree than any other consideration. When selecting your trees, specify that you want *true* dwarfing rootstock, *genetically* dwarfed, or miniature trees. Tell the nursery owner that you plan to espalier the trees.

Although most of us are limited when choosing the site that our trees will occupy, we must still try and provide them with the best location. A gentle east- or west-facing slope is ideal. Slopes facilitate both air and water drainage, and an east or west orientation ensures that the trees will receive at least their daily minimum requirement of 6 hours of direct sunlight. The type of soil is equally important. It should be well drained and reasonably fertile. Avoid heavy clay or sandy soils and sites with poor drainage. Work the soil deeply and incorporate plenty of organic matter to improve drainage and fertility.

You may be able to find trees that have been started in an espalier pattern, but probably you will have to start at the very beginning with a bare root—a one- or two-year-old whip. These should be planted as soon as the ground can be prepared in the spring. Let the roots soak in a bucket for 1 or 2 hours while you prepare the hole for the transplants as for other bare-root plants (see Blackberries, page 39). Make sure that the graft of the fruit stock rests 1 or 2 inches above the soil line. The soil can be mounded near the plant and then depressed into a well around the trunk. This helps to retain water, but can be dangerous in cold weather; if there is water in the well and it freezes, the trunk can freeze and damage the tender stem. Fill in the well before freezing weather.

Started espaliers are grown either in a container or with the rootball wrapped in burlap. Fiber pots can be planted with the tree if you observe the same precautions as for peat pots (see page 44). Other containers must be carefully removed. Burlap wrapped roots should have the top half of the burlap unwrapped and folded down before settling the plants into the planting hole.

After planting, water deeply and mulch around the tree, but leave bare the first few inches near the trunk. Wrap the trunk with plastic strips to protect from pests or lawn mowers, or paint the trunk with a white, water based, latex paint that has been diluted 50/50 with water to protect the bark from pest damage and from absorbing too much heat and splitting.

If planting a row of trees, position them so that the line runs north to south. Fruit-bearing spurs tend to form facing the light. An east to west wall of trees will produce nearly all of its fruit on the south side—something to remember if you are planning a property divider with a southerly neighbor.

PRUNING

Training producing fruit trees into a pattern requires an understanding of how they grow and how they set fruit. Each growing new branch will be covered with a variety of buds (apple, pear, plum, and apricot boughs will also sprout spurs). These short, new branches grow from established branches to produce fat buds that flower and set fruit. A terminal bud forms at the tip of each new branch. The terminal bud grows quickly, but removing it limits the growth of that branch and prompts more buds to form.

Leaf buds first appear as tiny, flattened triangles along the new branch. If the branch is cut just above a leaf bud, the bud's growth is stimulated. Flower buds of fruit spurs, the first to swell each spring, are much fatter than leaf buds. Flower buds blossom and set fruit, so do not remove them. When pruning, note the direction that the remaining buds are facing because that is the direction where future limbs will grow.

During late winter or early spring, while dormant branches are just beginning to bud, most traditional pruning takes place. This is the time for major wood removal for nonespaliered trees and shrubs, but most espalier pruning is carried out in snips over the length of the summer, which is much less stressful to the tree and less of a chore for the gardener.

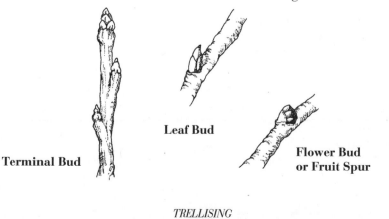

Leaf Bud

Terminal Bud

Flower Bud or Fruit Spur

It would be convenient if all fruit trees set fruit in the same way, but, unfortunately, it is not that simple. It is essential to know how a fruit tree develops its fruit before undertaking any pruning and risking the removal of fruiting wood or possible injury to the tree.

Apples and pears set fruit in the same way; they develop spurs from old, established branches. For this reason, they have become classical favorites for espalier since they can be trained into a permanent pattern and produce fruit from the same branches for decades. The spurs grow a little bigger each year; each one continues to produce for a decade or more. Be very careful not to injure the spurs during pruning or harvest.

Apricots and Japanese plums also produce spurs on older wood, but the spurs do not survive long. Most fruit forms on one-year-old branches. Pruning keeps a steady supply of new wood that comes to fruit in the next season.

Cherry trees are a challenge to espalier. There are two types with decidedly different growth habits. Sweet cherries grow large and tall, while sour (or pie) cherries bush out short and wide. Both types bear on spurs that begin forming on two-year-old wood.

Peaches and nectarines produce fruit on one-year-old wood, which once harvested never sets fruit again. Heavy pruning is necessary to keep new wood coming in order for the tree to set fruit.

While apples and pears may be trained to almost any shape imaginable, other fruit trees perform best if grown in a fan shape since this permits the most growth of new wood, while maintaining a recognizable pattern (see illustrations on page 96).

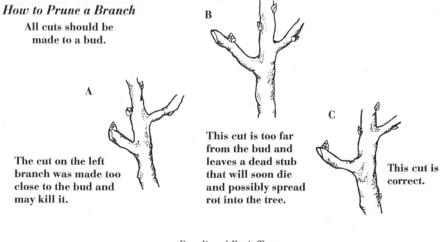

How to Prune a Branch
All cuts should be made to a bud.

B

A

The cut on the left branch was made too close to the bud and may kill it.

This cut is too far from the bud and leaves a dead stub that will soon die and possibly spread rot into the tree.

C

This cut is correct.

TRAINING

The graceful form of an espaliered tree is a testimonial to the gardener's dedication. Although it takes only a little effort, it takes *consistent* effort. Pruning, pinching, bending, propping, and tying must be tended to faithfully to maintain the pattern and to keep fruit production at its peak.

Trees may be espaliered to a wall, a fence, a wire, a wooden lattice trellis, or whatever arrangement meets your needs. When training on or near a wall or solid fence, always leave at least 6 inches between the tree trunk and the surface. This not only allows you to reach the wall if you need to, but also provides air circulation for the tree and a little room for pruning, pest control, and harvesting.

In Europe, it is common practice to grow espaliered trees alongside walls and fences. The reflected light and heat from the wall help to ripen the fruit as well as shelter the tree from inclement weather. But in areas where summer temperatures routinely top 90°F, this can prove disastrous because the extra heat can cook the fruit on the branches.

A typical espalier trellis, whether along a fence or out in the open, consists of either wood or wire horizontal supports that are held in place by sturdy posts or by a fence. Large eyebolts or floor flanges attach wires to walls. Attaching one end of each wire to a turnbuckle keeps the wire taut and straight. For any designs that include right angles, straight lines are mandatory. As with other trellises, use galvanized wire and galvanized nails or copper wire and nongalvanized nails. Wire should be fairly heavy. Ten-gauge copper wire or 3/16-inch, vinyl coated, tiller cable wire works well. You may also need additional supports for training the trunk and the vertical or angled cordons. Use bamboo or redwood stakes that are driven into the ground or tied to horizontal supports wherever needed.

For many espaliered tree patterns the first step is to train 2 opposing horizontal cordons from a short trunk. Cut back the top of the newly planted whip at the height that you wish the first cordons to form. This should fall somewhere between 1 to 2 feet high. As new shoots begin to form, choose the best 2 or 3 shoots and remove all others.

If you are training a design with only one set of horizontal arms, such as a single, horizontal cordon or a simple U shape (see illustrations on page 95), leave only 2 buds—each one to train along the trellis in either direction. If your design requires more than one horizontal level, such as a horizontal T (see illustration on page 95), trim all but the best 3 buds. The middle bud will be trained into the central leader, which is the main vertical trunk of the tree. Stake or tie the trunk so that it grows absolutely straight.

Guide the side shoots into position as they grow, and tie them to the wires. Bending the branches downward significantly slows their rate of growth. The growing limbs are flexible enough to do this gradually. Begin by positioning them in a 45° angle from the main trunk, and as they reach the desired length, bend them down to the wire in right angles with the trunk.

Stake or tie the central leader so that it rises straight up from the lower trunk. Once it reaches the height that you want for the second level of cordons, usually about 1½ feet, repeat the process of choosing, removing, and training buds. You may continue this pattern for years as the tree grows ever taller into orderly rows of limbs, or you may stop at any point and maintain the chosen height simply by retaining only 2 buds once the tree has reached the height that you want. Once the side branches reach the desired length, usually no more than 3 to 4 feet, head them back each year during early spring pruning.

Training Espaliered Trees

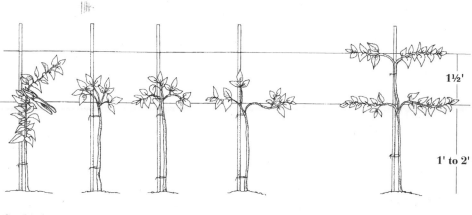

| Cut back the top of the new plant (first cordon). | New shoots will grow. | Choose 2 or 3 of the new shoots. Remove the other shoots. | Allow 1 center shoot to become the central leader trunk. Remove all other shoots on the horizontal branches. | In the following spring, start the second set of horizontal branches (second cordon) 1½' above the first shoot from the central leader. |

1½'

1' to 2'

The same principles apply in training Palmette Oblique, Palmette Verrier, Belgian Fence, and Losange patterns (see illustrations on pages 95 and 96). For Palmette Oblique, choose and train 3 buds until the tree reaches the desired height, but leave the buds at 45° angles rather than bending them down to right angles.

To train a Palmette Verrier or U-shaped espalier, you must bend the ends of the cordons upward after they have been trained horizontally. For a single U, this is done once the horizontal cordons reach about 10 inches in length. For a double or triple U, let the side branches grow until they are nearly as long as the desired width of the finished pattern before bending upward. At this point, carefully bend and tie the side branches to a vertical support. A general rule is to allow 16 inches between each vertical cordon for sufficient light, aeration, and fruit formation. As these first vertical cordons reach the point where the next U is to form, head them back and wait for new buds to form. Choose the best 2 buds and train them like a single U by tying them horizontally until they reach the point where the upward turn is desired.

The Palmette Verrier requires forethought in order to train the bottom U wide enough to allow for the smaller U's that will grow up within it. In the first year, allow the horizontal cordons to grow 36 to 46 inches long before bending them upward. In the following year, allow the second level of horizontal cordons to reach a length of 24 to 28 inches before tying them vertically. Finally, during the third season of training, the arms of the center U can be turned upward when they are from 8 to 10 inches long.

The intricate looking Belgian Fence and the fancier Losange variation are really very simple to train. Rather than many corners and turns on an individual tree, the effect comes from 1 or 2 branches of several trees that are trained in a row. The trees can line an existing fence or wall or can create a freestanding divider. Train the Belgian Fence by heading back each new tree as it reaches a height of about 18 inches and by training 2 buds in a V. This makes each tree look like a Y, but a planting of several in a row, 18 to 24 inches apart, will create the crisscross diamond pattern along its length.

Expanding upon the Belgian Fence creates the Losange. The trees must be spaced a little farther apart, about 24 to 48 inches, to allow room for the extra branches. Train like a Belgian fence until the angled limbs reach a length of about 16 inches; then head them back to produce buds. Choose the best buds that are facing upward and parallel to the original, angled cordon that is opposite it, and train according to the pattern.

The Arcure method produces a lovely, simple pattern of interconnecting arches (see illustration on page 96). It requires a trellis that is strung with wires every 16 to 18 inches to the desired height of the finished pattern. Like the last two methods, this also creates a freestanding fence. The difference, though, in the Arcure method begins at planting.

With the Arcure method, place the whips in the ground about 3 feet apart, each at a slight angle toward the right. After the tree has recovered from the shock of planting and has become somewhat established, pull the tip of the tree over into an arch, and tie it to the support. (You may need to stake and tie in several places to get just the right curve.) Pinch or snip off all the shoots that form until one shoot sprouts at the top center of the curve. This will form the next level of the pattern.

Late in the summer, bend this shoot into a curve in the opposite direction of the branch from which it is growing. Tie the tip of this arch to the base of the center shoot on the tree to its left. (The last tree to the left will have this cordon cut and trained in midarch.)

In the following season, choose 1 bud at the top center of the second level arch, and train it into a curve back toward the right. Again tie the tip of this arch to the base of its neighbor. Continue this pattern until the desired height is achieved. In the final year of training, remove all the shoots along the top curve, and tie the top curve to the base of the adjacent curve. Remember that once the cordons are bent downward, they tend to stop growing.

The natural tendency of the cordons is to grow vertically. This can be put to good use in a Gridiron pattern (see illustration on page 96). Train like a Palmette Verrier by beginning with two horizontal cordons that are bent upward as they reach the desired length. Along these cordons at regular intervals of 16 inches allow a few chosen buds to sprout vertically. Head these buds back once they reach the desired height, and prune them each spring.

Fans are generally an informal pattern and are trained either to a short trunk or from several stems (see illustrations on page 96). Be sure that the fan part of the design begins a few inches above the bud graft. This is done by cutting back the trunk of the young tree to only 6 to 8 inches and by allowing several buds to form. Train between 5 to 7 of these buds at various angles into the supports by using bamboo or wooden stakes that are tied to wires. Once the cordons have spread out, allow as many side branches to form as the tree can gracefully support.

APPLES

Apple lover John Chapman, better known in American history as Johnny Appleseed, sent westward-bound pioneers on their way with packets of dried, brown seeds. The trees that grew from these seeds made apples America's favorite, tree fruit. Apple trees grew throughout most of North America, and thanks to the diversity of cold-tolerant and low-chill varieties, they grow here still. Washington State, New York, and Michigan boast the finest apple orchards in the world.

VARIETIES

Approximately 1,000 different varieties of apples exist. Some ripen early, such as Lodi, Liberty, and Yellow Transparent, while others, such as Gravenstein, McIntosh, and Paulared, ripen somewhat later. Cortland, Empire, and Jonathan are midseason favorites, and are followed seasonally by Red and Golden Delicious, Mutsu, Granny Smith, and Rome Beauty.

Apple varieties are often divided according to how they are best used—fresh or cooked. Those best suited for fresh eating are sweet and crisp. Red Delicious is the classic example, but Liberty and Jonathan are also favorites. Cooking apples are often tart and firm. Lodi, Granny Smith, and Northern Spy are ideal for cooking or baking. Many varieties, including Gravenstein, Paulared, Cortland, and Empire, have won favor as dual purpose apples and are excellent fresh or cooked.

Although we often picture a perfectly ripe apple as shiny red, many varieties stay green even when ripe. Others may fade to yellow perhaps with just a faint blush. Lodi, Granny Smith, Mutsu, and Golden Delicious never see a hint of red. Gravenstein and McIntosh blush red over a yellow background.

Apple varieties have been developed to tolerate temperature extremes and to ward off diseases. Red Baron and Regent are extra hardy, while Anna, Ein Shemer, and Winter Banana set fruit with very little, winter chill. Liberty is prized for its resistance to fire blight, scab, mildew, and cedar rust as well as for its tasty, versatile fruit.

Rootstocks differ nearly as much as fruit stocks. When selecting, ask which dwarfing rootstock is grafted to the fruiting variety. For most conditions, M9 or M26 rootstocks are recommended, except for in poor soils. In soils that impair growth, such as heavy clay or sand, opt for MM106, a vigorous growing variety. Trees classified as miniatures are genetically dwarfed, which means that they grow small on their own roots, smaller than most grafter dwarfs.

SITE & SOIL REQUIREMENTS

The home that all apple trees dream of is a sunny slope. Most trees require a winter chill to set fruit in the following spring, but their needs vary. Good drainage is important, and light loam or gravelly soil is preferred. Apple trees will tolerate a range of soils, however, with heavy clay or sand as the least satisfactory. The trees draw three times as much nitrogen and potassium from the soil as phosphorus as well as drawing out small amounts of trace elements, such as boron, copper, magnesium, manganese, and zinc. Like most fruit trees, apple trees do best in soil that is slightly acidic with a pH range of 6.5 to 6.8. Soils that are well amended with compost or rotted manures should supply all these needs.

ESPALIER DESIGN

Apples are the darling of espalier gardeners for good reason. They not only offer an astounding variety of tempting fruit, but also their growth habit allows them to bear for years within the confines of an espalier design. They can successfully be trained to almost any design, but yields are highest when branches are trained to a 45° angle. Palmette Verrier, Belgian Fence, or a row of single cordon, 45°-angled trees all feature such branches (see illustrations on pages 95 and 96). In all cases, the cordons should be spaced 18 to 24 inches apart to allow for air circulation and fruit production.

GROWING TIPS

A well-tended apple tree can produce for 50 years or more, beginning the second or third season. All that it requires is minimum attention to its basic needs. Adequate water is a fundamental requirement. In times of drought, be sure to soak the base of the tree every 7 to 10 days. A garden hose that is left to drip for 1 hour or more will provide plenty of water to thirsty roots. Nutrient requirements can usually be met with an occasional top dressing of compost or rotted manure. Do not apply the top dressing after late spring because this encourages vegetative growth that may not mature before frost and leaves the growth vulnerable to winter injury.

Pollination is another basic need; without it, nothing else will cause an apple tree to fruit. Most varieties are self-sterile—they require a tree of another variety to provide pollen. The pollinator variety must be one that flowers at the same time as well as provides adequate amounts of pollen. Check with your tree supplier about which varieties will cross-pollinate with those that you select. Once the trees are in flower, it is up to insects, primarily bees, to get the job done. Beekeeping is a valuable sideline for any gardener or fruit tree grower.

A 3-inch thick mulch around the base of the tree will conserve moisture, cut down on weed competition, and keep the tree's roots from enduring extreme temperature fluctuations. Mulches should be pulled away from the trunk in the winter since they are prime hideouts for rodents.

Aside from the pinching and snipping that are ordained by espalier, little pruning is in order. Apple trees, however, benefit from fruit thinning. In the early summer when the fruit is about the size of marbles, there is a natural fruit drop—nature's way of lightening the load. Just after this drop is the best time to thin fruit to about 6 inches between each developing apple. This allows bigger, better tasting fruit to form.

PESTS & DISEASES

Spoiled by perfect looking supermarket fruit, many people are not happy with the appearance of homegrown unless it too is sprayed for pests and diseases. The most prevalent pests are the codling moth, which causes the proverbial wormy apple, San Jose scale, aphids, leaf rollers, and apple maggots. Try hanging Red Sphere Traps (see Appendix II) to catch the adult flying, codling moths. Keep scale in check with a dormant oil spray that should be applied late in the winter. Employ insect predators, such as ladybugs and praying mantis, and maintain strict standards of clean cultivation to cut down on other pests.

Rabbits or voles can destroy young trees by nibbling away the bark, especially in the winter. Wrap the trunks, and apply a repellent, such as Predator Scent to discourage them (see Appendix II).

Several diseases trouble apple trees, but the worst are scab and fire blight. Scab is instantly recognized as scabby, discolored spots on fruit and leaves; Liberty, Prima, and Macfree are resistant. Fire blight blackens twigs and small fruit as if they were actually burned. There is no cure and infected limbs should be removed.

RIPE & READY

Apples ripen to perfection right on the branch. With some varieties, it can be difficult to tell just when they have reached that point. Empire develops a full red color weeks before it is ready for harvest. What about those others that develop little or no red color?

The best test is a taste test. A ripe apple has a characteristic flavor and texture according to its variety. The fruit should reach an appropriate size for the type of tree. When perfectly ripe, the fruit will separate from the spur just as the stem is bent upward. Always be careful when harvesting apples not to damage the spur or to bruise the fruit. Split the apple open to check for another sign of ripeness; in most apple varieties, the seeds will have changed from white to brown.

Apples contain vitamin K, fiber, and pectin. Fresh off the tree, they are a delight. They are also delicious when they are dehydrated for healthful snacks, tasty additions to cold cereal, or bread and muffin recipes. Applesauce is a time-honored favorite of young and old, and what could be more American than apple pie?

PEARS

Pears are closely related to apples and are the next best choice for an espaliered fruit tree. Like apples, they bear their fruit on long-lived spurs that lend themselves well to the restricted form of an espalier. They can be finicky trees to grow and often get into the habit of biennial bearing, which produces a bumper crop one year and next to nothing the next year. But their delicate blossoms and sumptuous fruit make them worth any peculiarities that they may exhibit.

VARIETIES

Most people when they think pear, think Bartlett. It has been the most commonly grown pear in this country and, by familiarity, the standard by which others are judged. The pears are large sized and good looking, but bland and of only fair quality. For anyone who wants a familiar pear,

Bartlett may seem like the logical choice, but there are so many more.

In general, pears can be classified as sweet or tart with varying degrees of intensity. Flavors range from Bartlett bland to Seckel spicy with a hint of strawberry or pineapple. The outside of the fruit is always yellowish with or without speckling or a blush, like Moonglow, but there is always a range in the texture and color of the flesh. Bartlett is lightly green tinged; Flemish Beauty is white; Tyson is yellow; Josephine De Malines is reddish. The texture may be fine or coarse, juicy or dry, buttery, crisp, or tough. Some are more resistant to disease than others; Keiffer and Tyson are among the most resistant, and Bartlett is among the more susceptible.

Some varieties ripen early, such as Clapp's Favorite and Moonglow, while others ripen later, such as D'Anjou, Bosc, Duchess, and Keiffer. Bartlett is a midseason variety.

Bosc is an exceptionally fragrant pear with an elongated shape, crisp texture, and good flavor. It is a favorite among home growers since it is also one of the best-suited varieties for dwarfing.

Like apples, most pears are self-sterile, which means a pollinator variety must be planted nearby. Starking Delicious is a good tasting, disease-resistant pear that is available in dwarf form and acts as a pollinator for many other varieties. Seckel, Bosc, and Flemish Beauty usually require no outside pollination.

Clapp's Favorite is hardy enough to be recommended for cold climates, while Mericourt originated and excels in the South. Keiffer requires little winter chill, but can take both hot and cold temperature extremes better than most, which makes it a widely adaptable variety.

SITE & SOIL REQUIREMENTS

Pears are more choosy about climate and soil than almost any other fruit tree. They are less cold tolerant than apples, but less heat tolerant than peaches. They thrive in damp, overcast regions, like the coastal Pacific Northwest. Like other fruit trees, they are susceptible to late frosts and prefer a sloping site that sweeps cold air downwind.

The dwarf varieties, unlike the standard trees, are shallow rooted, which makes them more susceptible to extreme summer heat or deep frosts. They are shallow rooted because they are grafted to quince roots. Ask for those varieties that are grown on Quince A or Quince C rootstock.

Pears also require fertile soil, which makes the garden a perfect site.

They can tolerate more water retentive ground than most other fruit trees and do well in heavy loam or clay. The light loam or gravelly soils that apples adore, pears abhor. If forced to grow in poorly suited soils, the tree will retaliate by producing tough, bitter, gritty fruit.

ESPALIER DESIGN

Pears are just as versatile in espalier design as apples. They can fruit in a trained pattern for many years, beginning in their second or third season. Designs that incorporate vertical cordons will provide the highest fruit production. A single, double, or triple U design, a Palmette Oblique, or the Gridiron are all well suited to pears (see illustrations on pages 95 and 96.)

GROWING TIPS

Finicky pears demand their share of coddling, or they will set poor quality, intermittent, or no fruit. A healthy dose of compost or rotted manure each spring will give them a timely wake-up call to get them growing and preparing to fruit. They require about 35 inches of annual rainfall and will suffer from a lack of water. Regular irrigation and thick mulching are often necessary. Heavy mulch will also protect those shallow quince roots from the summer heat. The mulch must be pulled away from the tree trunk for the winter because pests will take advantage of the protective cover that it affords. Pears are also vulnerable to frost damage in the winter and may need to be wrapped or covered for protection.

The best pears that any variety has to offer are the biggest fruit that the tree can produce. To insure large, flavorful fruit, thin the developing pears shortly after the natural drop to a spacing of about 6 inches apart. Since pear trees can get into a habit of overproducing one year and underproducing the next year, fruit thinning is also important to let the tree conserve energy for the following season.

PESTS & DISEASES

Pears suffer many of the same ills as apples. Late season varieties may be bothered by codling moths. Pear psylla and San Jose scale dwell in the tree bark and can be stopped with a late winter, dormant oil spray. Tiny mites can also trouble pears and can also be dealt with by a dormant oil spray or by a fall spraying of oil and lime sulfur.

Pear Public Enemy Number One is fire blight, a bacterial disease that in susceptible varieties seems ever present. It leaves the trees with a characteristic burned appearance and can be deadly. The constant summer pinching that is required to develop and maintain the espalier is very helpful in controlling the disease, and any noticeably infected branches should be immediately removed and burned. Fire blight is much more serious in pears than in apples and calls for vigilance and quick action. Scab may also bother pears, but can be avoided by planting resistant varieties.

RIPE & READY

Ah, the pleasures of tree ripened fruit—except in this case. Pears just had to be different.

A tree ripened pear is most likely to be mushy and brown and will not keep for ten minutes off the branch. To get the best flavor and texture, harvest underripe pears. Pick the fruit once it has reached full size and has just begun to show a hint of mature color. A good test is to tip the fruit up from the stem, and if it is ready to pick, it will come free easily.

Be very gentle when picking pears—the slightest bump will bruise this sensitive fruit. Bruises quickly degenerate to rot, which ruins the fruit for storage. Store only perfect fruit in a cool place in shallow, airtight containers until a few days before serving. They will need a few days at room temperature to ripen to sweet perfection.

Many varieties are good canned and by dehydrating ripened pears, their rich, unique flavor is concentrated. They are a good source of vitamins A and K and dietary fiber.

CHERRIES

Cherry trees are beautiful enough to grow just for looks. Whether in blossom or dripping with fruit, they exude a luxurious grace and radiance all their own. They are also forgiving—another attractive quality in a homegrown fruit tree. Many varieties can tolerate a wide range of soils, climates, and drought. They are not, however, especially cooperative to espalier. Their fruit is set on short-lived spurs, which means they need more new growth than apples or pears.

VARIETIES

Pop a sweet cherry into your mouth, then smile and spit. Pop a sour cherry and you may have to pucker a little, but the sour, or pie, varieties of cherries will make you smile with their easy natures. While sweet cherries can be very choosy about soils and climates and are susceptible to pests and diseases, sour cherries seem nearly impervious to all of these conditions.

Good dwarf sweet varieties include Stella Sweet, which also is self-pollinating unlike other sweet varieties, and Royal Ann, a classic. Sweet cherries range from nearly black, like in Bing, or in the bright red of Starkrimson, to the blushing yellow of Royal Ann and Rainier or the golden yellow of Stark Gold.

Montmorency is the established favorite of pie cherries. It is hardy and self-pollinating, like North Star, a genetically dwarfed, disease-resistant cherry. Meteor is a genetic dwarf sweet variety that grows to only 10 feet tall. It is self-pollinating and fares well in a range of climates.

Duke cherries blend the best of sweet and sour cherries. They produce hardy, vigorous trees that require cross-pollination. The drupe fruits look like sweet cherries, but taste more like sour cherries. Royal Duke is an excellent variety.

Some controversy previously existed regarding dwarfing rootstocks. Mazzard roots produce full-sized, vigorous, long-lived trees, while trees grafted to Mahaleb roots were dwarfed and began to fail after 10 or 12 years. The best choice for espalier are the genetically dwarfed, or miniature varieties. Given a standard rootstock, cherry trees can rival the biggest shade trees for size.

ESPALIER DESIGN

All stone fruits, cherries included, are best suited to a fan-shaped espalier (see illustration on page 96). This design is less formal than the traditional designs and allows for continual introduction of new branches without ruining the effect of the pattern. Once spurs have finished fruiting, they and the old branches that they occupy can be removed and newcomers can be trained to take their place.

GROWING TIPS

The best thing that you can do to insure a happy sweet cherry tree is to choose a variety that is well suited to your area. Sweet cherries require much less winter chill than their sour cousins, and they blossom early, which makes them vulnerable to late spring frosts. Sour cherries, on the other hand, cannot perform without a significant winter chill. They blossom late, which makes spring cold snaps unimportant. The requirements for the Duke varieties fall between sweets and sours.

Cherries like attention. Regular soil cultivation increases yields and tree vigor. Feeding is rarely necessary, but working compost into the soil never hurts. Heavy summer rains may cause fruit to crack and cause subsequent rotting in sweet cherries. Consider planting a thirsty ground cover near the base of your cherry trees if your area is prone to summer downpours.

Cherries require no fruit thinning and the openness of the espalier will make harvesting a simple pleasure. Sour cherries, known for their dense foliage, benefit from the improved air circulation that espalier allows.

Sweet cherry trees are usually sold as one-year-old whips and sour cherry trees as two year olds. They begin producing in 2 or 3 years and may continue for over half a century.

PESTS & DISEASES

Birds are a major problem for cherry growers. If you let them, they will harvest your entire crop for you. Espaliered trees are easily protected with bird netting that is draped over the trees just as the cherries begin to color. The birds are not interested until the cherries are ripe.

Cherries suffer less from insect damage than other fruit trees, but there are still some bugs to watch for. Nothing spoils a handful of warm, sweet, freshly picked cherries more than one little, squirmy, cherry fruit maggot. Pear slugs and aphids may also visit sweet cherries, and tent caterpillars will set up camp in any available cherry tree.

Diseases are more common in sweet cherries, but may also occur in the sour varieties. Brown rot and cherry leaf spot thrive in warm, wet weather and target sweet cherries. Yellows and ring spot virus complex may also affect sweet cherries, but are more common problems in sour cherries. Trees that are transplanted into soil that is infected with the fungus verticillium wilt will fail within the first 2 years.

RIPE & READY

You do not even need a ladder! Dwarf cherries are almost as easy to pick as they are to eat. Just pluck from the branch and plunk them into a pail. Taste and color are the best indicators of ripeness. Keep an eye on any unprotected trees because the attention that they will get from birds is a sure sign of ripe cherries.

All cherries are a good source of vitamins A and K, but sour cherries provide ten times as much vitamin A as sweet cherries. Firm-fleshed sweet cherries will keep in the refrigerator in plastic bags for up to 3 weeks, but soft sour cherries last only a few days. Cherries can be canned, either pitted or unpitted, or processed in preserves and pie fillings. Cherry flavored syrups and sorbets are sensational.

APRICOTS, PEACHES & NECTARINES

Gardeners often shy away from the larger stone fruits because of the persnickety reputations that apricots, peaches, and nectarines have acquired. While it is true that they need more attention than other fruit trees in pruning, frost protection, and pest and disease control, the spectacular displays of limb-smothering blossoms and generous offerings of delectable, sun ripened fruit make up for the extra effort. With a little special treatment, an espaliered apricot, peach, or nectarine tree will make you proud.

VARIETIES

There are few distinctions to be made with apricots. They may be freestone (freely releasing the pit) or not. Some are more cold tolerant than others, although all are hardier than peaches or nectarines. There are also some differences in pollination requirements. Royal and Moorpark are favorites and Floragold is a genetic dwarf that grow only 6 to 8 feet tall and bears an early, heavy crop. Goldcot is both hardy and self-pollinating.

Peaches vary in color, ripening time, hardiness, chill requirement, and resistance to disease, but they all produce round, fuzzy, melt-in-your-mouth fruit. Nectarines are closely related to peaches. They vary somewhat in appearance, but the rich aroma and melting, peachlike flavor are unmistakable. With little else to set them apart, nectarines are really just bald peaches.

For a long time, the standard by which peaches were judged was Elberta, a late season variety that produces large, round, golden fruit with a red blush. Part of the reason that Elberta was so revered was that it adapts well to a range of soils and temperate climates. Redhaven is another adaptable peach and is preferred by many over Elberta. Deep red fruit with firm, yellow flesh that does not brown when it is exposed to air also makes it a favorite. Both are available on dwarfing peach or almond rootstock. Honey Babe, Sunburst, and Garden Sun are genetic dwarfs; they ripen in June, July, and August, respectively, and are self-pollinating.

Nectarines also vary in ripening times, hardiness, and disease resistance. Sungold and Sunred ripen early and need only moderate-to-low winter chill. Mericrest ripens in midseason, is very hardy, and offers some disease resistance. Gold Mine is an old favorite, late ripener. Gold Mine is not easy to find on dwarfing rootstock unfortunately, but its quality makes a do-it-yourself, grafting project a worthwhile endeavor. Genetic dwarfs that grow to only about 6 feet tall are also available.

SITE & SOIL REQUIREMENTS

Like other fruit trees, apricots, peaches, and nectarines benefit from the air and water drainage that accompany a slope. They demand good drainage and a soil that will hold warmth. Rocky, gravelly, or sandy soils are ideal. Clay and loam, if well drained and deep, will be politely tolerated by peaches and nectarines, but apricots do best in a deep, sandy loam. The soil, however, does not have to be especially fertile. These trees draw heavily on potassium, calcium, and magnesium, but too much nitrogen prompts lots of vegetation that often gets caught by frost before it matures.

Usually you cannot make a mistake when you decide where to place your tree if you are in a good peach-growing area. If you are not in such an area, you should remember that the foremost need of a peach is warmth. They are temperamental trees that demand a sufficient winter chill and a warm summer. Low spots, corners, or flat sites may collect cold, still air that threatens the trees with freezing in the winter or frost damage during flowering. In colder climates, some type of shelter, such as espaliering along a northeast facing wall or fence, is greatly appreciated.

ESPALIER DESIGN

Apricots, peaches, and nectarines bear fruit on one-year-old wood. Once a *portion* of a limb has set fruit, it is finished for the life of the tree. This keeps the fruit developing on the outside of the tree where it receives the most light. In order to keep new wood coming, it also makes heavy pruning a necessity. This limits the espalier design to either an informal shape or a fan (see illustrations on page 96). The espalier will amply reward your efforts due to the openness of the tree and the constant summer pinching, pruning, and attention that all promote good health and great harvests.

GROWING TIPS

Plant an apricot, peach, or nectarine variety that is suited to your region. Give it the best possible location. Train it, prune it, spray for disease, check for bugs, and then get to work.

These trees do demand that you earn their rewards. Work the soil regularly to discourage pests. Water judiciously. Although they despise soggy soil, a dry spell at anytime that fruit is on the tree may leave you with puny peaches. Leave a dripping hose at the base of the tree for 1 to 2 hours every 10 days to saturate the soil. Allow the soil to nearly dry in between waterings. A thick mulch can help the tree through hot spells by buffering the roots from the heat as well as maintaining constant moisture. Fertilizing is not a high priority, but a top dressing of aged manure or compost early in the spring will replace those nutrients that the tree has absorbed.

With peaches and nectarines, fruit thinning is very important for the best tasting fruit. It also helps prevent the tree from expending too much energy or drawing too many resources from the soil. Following the natural fruit drop that occurs in early summer, cull all but the best developing fruit from each cluster. A spacing of 4 to 6 inches between fruit is perfect, but it is the overall load that the tree bears that is most important.

Frost protection is especially important in the spring when the flowers are in bloom. Just one cold night can wipe out an entire crop of unsuspecting apricots, peaches, or nectarines. A layer of mulch, at least 6 inches deep, can fool the trees into flowering a week or more later than they would naturally flower. Mulch the tree in late winter, while the soil is still frozen and the tree is dormant. The roots will keep cooler under the mulch as spring temperatures rise. The result is that flowering is delayed until the tree "thinks" that it is warm enough—perhaps long enough to stave off that last spring frost. Of course, other factors also induce a tree to flower, such as the duration and angle of sunlight, but any advantage is worth taking.

Given their delicate constitutions, just a nip of frost can be disastrous. The closer that the tree is to blossoming, the more sensitive it is to cold. Fruit buds die at temperatures of 20°F. Often flowers succumb if the temperature falls to 26°F or lower, and once the petals drop, a low of 28°F can kill the fruit. Place large stones around the base of the tree after the tree flowers; they will absorb heat during the day and later release it into the chilly night air.

Tender wood growth that has not matured before frost is also susceptible to cold damage and to subsequent invasion by disease organisms. Try to avoid this havoc by not feeding the tree after early spring and by removing any tender shoots after the first frost.

PESTS & DISEASES

Many insects annoy apricots, peaches, and nectarines, but only a relative few are bent on destruction. These trees do not take kindly to any sort of insult, however, and will fairly swoon in their discontent. The worst offenders are aphids, peach tree borers, plum curculio, and scale. Of these, peach tree borers are the greatest threat. They tunnel into the base of the trunk and feed beneath the bark; this can kill a young tree and demands immediate action. The standard treatment is to seek the borers out and gouge them with a sharp knife. An injectable form of *Bacillus thuringiensis* (Bt) (see Appendix II) is also available. Plum curculio is especially damaging to nectarines, but espaliered trees have an advantage since these shady bugs avoid sunlight. Maintaining an open espalier may spare the fruit.

Apricot, peach, and nectarine trees are so beset by diseases that most people resort to chemical warfare. Bacterial spot is a serious disease that causes the most problems in the warm, moist weather that the trees prefer. A worse disease is brown rot, a fungus that directly affects fruit and spreads quickly. Many varieties are resistant to these ailments, but others, such as cankers and yellows, must be cut out as soon as they are detected. The mysterious X-Disease is spread by leafhoppers and can kill the entire tree above the soil line, while it leaves the roots alive to send up more diseased shoots.

RIPE & READY

Peaches and nectarines will begin to treat you to their juicy, golden treasures during the second season after planting. Production will be in full swing by the fourth or fifth year. Apricots may lag a year behind, but are well worth the wait.

Tree ripened peaches are incomparable to anything that you have purchased in a supermarket. The flesh is soft and sweet and melts like butter when you bite into it. Peaches may be picked before they reach this stage as are market peaches. If allowed to fully ripen on the vine, peaches do not stay fresh for long. If picked just before they are ripe, they can be kept in cold storage for up to 2 weeks as they continue to ripen.

You may wait until the first few fruits drop from the trees or give a hanging apricot or peach a touch test to see if it is ready to pick. If the sides give to a light pressure between the index finger and thumb, tip it sideways with a twist. It should break free easily. Take pains when picking these delicate fruits since a barely noticeable bruise will become a rotten spot. Nectarines demand even more delicate handling because the naked fruit is softer and more prone to bruising.

Apricots are very high in vitamin A and contain twice as much of this vitamin as their nearest competition—nectarines. They are superb in desserts or made into nectar or syrup. They are commonly halved and dehydrated for a sunny, nutritious snack. Peaches are also a good source of vitamin A. They are a special, summer treat when eaten fresh out of hand, in salads, or with strawberries and cream for a decadent dessert. They are a favorite for cobblers, are wonderful seasoned and canned, and make a rare, sweet treat when dehydrated. Green peaches can be soaked in brine and pickled like giant green olives. Nectarines have a richer flavor than peaches and top them for vitamin A and K content. They are best eaten fresh, but can be used in the same ways as peaches.

PLUMS

No tree fruit is more cosmopolitan than plums. With few exceptions, any garden in the continental United States can harbor some type of plum tree. Their sweet succulence is an easy reward for any gardener.

VARIETIES

With 2,000 or more different types, no fruit rivals the plum for sheer variety. They are divided into several groups. The most commonly grown, plum trees in this country are the self-pollinating European and cross-pollinating Japanese types. Some varieties, also called plum/prunes, mature into fruit with enough sugar and solid flesh to form a usable product when dried for storage. Italian Prune and French Prune are worth the effort of drying.

European plums include the egg shaped, dark blue-violet varieties, Stanley, Sugar, and Italian Prune. Other European plums, like the bright Yellow Egg, Green Gage, and French Prune that matures from red to nearly black, show more of a color range. Damson is an old, European variety that bears exceptionally juicy fruits that are prized for making jellies, juice, and preserves.

Japanese plum trees bloom earlier in the spring than the Europeans, which makes them less cold tolerant. They produce large, round fruits in colors ranging from the deep maroon of Burbank and Redheart and the purple of Santa Rosa to the dainty blush of Ember and the shiny yellow of Shiro.

There are many varieties that are native to the United States and prosper in their particular regions, and there are those that have been bred for special areas. Ember and Underwood are especially hardy and favored by northern growers.

Most plums are dwarfed onto apricot, Nanking cherry, or native rootstocks. Although plum trees do not reach the grand sizes of some other fruit trees, it is still important to request dwarf stock when you are planning to espalier plum trees.

SITE & SOIL REQUIREMENTS

Like peaches, plums do best in a slightly protected area or on a gentle slope. A north facing slope is often recommended for northern growers because the cooler, spring air may help to delay the early blooming that is so susceptible to frost.

Soil preferences vary with the type of plum tree. European plums favor clay. Damson plums revel in the heaviest soils. Almost any type of soil with good drainage can support some type of plum tree.

ESPALIER DESIGN

Neither European or Japanese plums are particularly well suited to espalier because of their fruit-bearing habits. Japanese plums generally fruit on spurs that are grown on new wood, while most of the other varieties bear on short-lived spurs and shoots of older wood. Japanese plums tend to send up many vertical branches and will bear best in designs that incorporate vertical or near vertical cordons. An informal espalier or fan shape are the easiest to maintain (see illustrations on page 96). Vertical cordon patterns, such as the Palmette Oblique, U designs, or the Gridiron, are also appropriate for plums, but may prove more challenging. (See illustrations on pages 95 and 96.)

GROWING TIPS

There is a plum tree for you! Virtually every garden in the continental United States can successfully grow some type of plums. Most European varieties are quite hardy, but do require a minimum winter chill to set fruit. Check with your local nursery owner for trees that will thrive in your area.

Almost all native and European varieties are self-pollinating, but many Japanese plum trees require an additional variety for pollination. Even those that are not dependent on cross-pollination perform better with the benefit of outside pollen. One of the best things that you can do for a plum tree is to give it pollen compatible company.

Except for the Japanese varieties, plum trees do not often require fruit thinning. Given the larger sized plum that they produce, Japanese plums, however, should be thinned to a spacing of 4 to 6 inches between the developing fruit. This not only produces larger more perfect plums, but also reduces the risk of overloaded branches breaking from the excess weight.

A midsummer application of compost that is worked into the soil will be welcomed by a heavily taxed tree. Keep the soil worked to disrupt weeds and insects. Mulch to conserve water, to smother weeds, and to protect the roots in hot weather.

PESTS & DISEASES

The plum curculio is one of the most universal pests of plums and related trees. The wormy larvae infest and ruin the fruit. A simple old-time remedy is to shake the larvae out of the tree onto a sheet spread beneath the tree during early morning, while they are still too lethargic to get away. Feed them to the chickens, or dunk them in a pail of water and kerosene.

Aphids, scale, and tent caterpillars may also lay claim to plum trees. A blast of cold water, dormant oil sprays, and pruning shears, in that order, will take care of these pests.

Happily, diseased plum trees are the exception rather than the norm. Fungal disease, such as black knot and brown rot, are among the most persistent ills. Black knot is a serious threat that will also affect cherry trees.

Swollen and knotted twigs and branches should be removed and destroyed immediately. Brown rot tends to favor the native and Japanese varieties; the European varieties are highly resistant to brown rot. Leaf spot occurs occasionally, and powdery mildew flourishes under warm, moist conditions. Espaliered fruit trees are much less susceptible—thanks to their improved air circulation.

RIPE & READY

Plum trees begin bearing in their third year and continue bearing for nearly 20 more years. Plums tend to ripen in waves rather than all at once, and different varieties begin ripening in different parts of the season. The plum harvest can last from midsummer to frost.

Plums are ready for picking after they have reached the full color for their variety and after hard flesh has softened enough to spring back when touched. They are not nearly as prone to bruising as peaches or nectarines. Pick by firmly grasping the fruit and snapping it free.

To truly appreciate a plum that is fresh from the tree, it must be completely ripe. Picked too soon, it will have an astringent, lip-puckering tang. Slightly unripe fruit can be processed in jams and preserves, but they will not get sweeter once they are off the tree.

Ripe plums can be kept refrigerated for up to 2 weeks and can be canned or dehydrated into prunes if they are of a suitable variety. Plums and prunes are nutritious as well as delicious and contain lots of vitamins A and K. Dried prunes are also high in iron.

ORNAMENTAL VINES

Many of the fruits and vegetables that have been discussed so far can serve double duty. Not only do trellised cucumbers or beans supply you with a bounty of fresh vegetables, but also they can be trained to hide a less-than-picturesque compost pile, a rusty storage tank, or other crops. They also can create a privacy screen, windbreak, or noise buffer. Espaliered trees can provide a living fence or a boundary line. Although many vines may not put food on the table, their harvest is one of aesthetics.

Simply for their beauty and fragrance, climbing vines can transform a common plot into an enchanted retreat. Sweet perfumes, wafting along warm summer breezes, seduce the senses of lucky passersby, while bright, bold, or delicate blossoms refresh the soul. While serving the most mundane purpose, a trellis that is loaded with foliage and blooms is an elegant statement. Birds and bees often find them irresistible and flock to your garden and linger to perform their vital tasks of pollination, pest control, and gardener amusement.

CLEMATIS

Few plants can rival the brilliant splendor of a clematis in bloom. Masses of brightly colored blossoms almost obscure the trellis. Treated properly, they will grow vigorously and quickly will cover a trellis in a single season. They do require attention to their demands, which makes them somewhat of a challenge. But once these challenges are met successfully, growing clematis is a most rewarding experience.

VARIETIES

Clematis come in nearly 300 varieties with a range of colors and flowering habits. A garden corner that is stocked with an assortment of clematis can be kept in bloom from late spring until freezing weather. Colors range from pure white to blue, purple, red, and pink with some combinations of colors. Some produce enormous blossoms that are 5 to 6 inches across. Deep pink Hagley Hybrid, ruby red Ernest Markham, white Henry I, and deep purple Jackmanii are just a few examples. Others boast a profusion of more delicate blooms. Some are richly scented, such as Japanese Paniculata, while others rely solely on their considerable eye appeal.

Clematis varieties can be distinguished from one another according to how and when they flower. Garden catalogues swell with varieties that bloom early and late and with many that flower throughout the summer. Most of the early bloomers also put on a somewhat less dramatic, fall show before retiring for the winter.

It is important to understand the type of flowering habit of your clematis. Some bear their glorious blossoms on one-year-old wood. To prune them back severely is a mistake that can cost the entire next season's flower show. Early flowering varieties, such as the double white Duchess of Edinburgh and the double silvery blue Belle of Woking, are generally those that blossom on old wood. Summer flowering types, such as Jackmanii and Paniculata, blossom from wood of the current season's growth. They can be cut back to within 1 foot of the ground early each spring and still can come up flowering.

SITE & SOIL REQUIREMENTS

For all their beauty, clematis demand some special treatment. They will thrive in full sun, but only if mulch or low growing, ground cover is provided to keep their roots cool. They will do well in partial shade, but must have at least a half day of sunlight, preferably with an eastern or western exposure.

Clematis have a decided preference for alkaline (pH 8+) soil. Their deep roots require porous, fertile soil with excellent moisture retention.

PLANTING

When setting out a new clematis plant, be sure that the soil has first passed the alkaline test. Most soils tend to be neutral to acid. Check first, and if necessary, work in lime to raise the pH level.

Dig the hole deep enough so that the plant can be set in about 2 inches deeper than it grew in the nursery or only 1 inch deeper in heavy soils. Stake the new plant, or provide it with a trellis from the start since the young stems are brittle and fragile. Prune the new vine to the lowest pair of healthy buds, and water well.

TRELLISING

There is at least one variety of clematis to grace any trellis. Those that bloom in the spring on one-year-old wood tend to run only 6 to 8 feet long, while those that bloom on new wood in the summer often sport vines from 25 to 30 feet in length. Trellises for the longer vines must be sturdy enough to support their weight.

Clematis can be trained onto arbors, along fences, up walls, or anywhere that you want a dazzling show of color. Training the vines onto an arbor with a horizontal support satisfies their desire for sun drenched foliage and their need for cool roots; the canopy of green and color provides shade for the base of the plant (see illustration on page 28).

GROWING TIPS

Keep clematis vines pruned according to their flowering habit. Summer bloomers should be cut back in the late winter to early spring while they are dormant. They can be pruned to the lowest pair of healthy flower buds on each vine. Spring-flowering varieties that flower on old wood should be cut back in the spring to about half their length. Find a strong pair of flower buds, and clip just ahead of them. These spring-flowering vines will need a second pruning after they finish flowering. At the second pruning, remove about one-quarter of the old growth, and cut no closer than 18 inches from the ground. Other clematis varieties also flower from shoots that develop on old wood. After flowering, these shoots should be cut back to two sets of flower buds. Be sure to check how your varieties develop.

Always keep the plants well watered because they cannot tolerate thirst. Work in compost, rotted cow manure, or bonemeal in the spring before the plant flowers to boost the blooms. Do this carefully without disturbing the roots, and mound the enriched soil up around the base of the plant. Clematis climb by means of coiling leaf stems and need little if any encouragement to amble upwards.

PESTS & DISEASES

Clematis fall prey to very few pests and diseases. The clematis borer, however, may stunt or kill branches as they hollow them out. Blister beetles, scale, and nematodes may also target these lovely plants. Although hand picking is a good way to combat many bugs, forget it with blister beetles; they get their name from caustic secretions that burn the skin. Stop scale with a dormant oil spray, and try to avoid nematode infested soil.

The major disease threat to clematis is wilt. Once infected, the plant cannot be spared, but must be cut out below the soil line and burned.

IVY

Ivy covered walls possess a formal elegance that no bare brick wall ever could approach. They impose images of scholars or royal knights. So appealing are the gently lobed shapes of ivy leaves, they have been incorporated into the works of artists and sculptors throughout the ages. But to be more practical, if you have something to hide, cover it with ivy.

VARIETIES

Many types of ivy are cultivated both vertically to cover trellises and horizontally for ground cover. The most familiar are the English Ivy and the Boston Ivy, which is not a true ivy. True English Ivy is native to Asia and North Africa and has been cultivated for centuries. Heart shaped, slightly lobed leaves grow to 4 inches across and cover vines up to 90 feet long. This is the classic, leaf shape that one sees so often in artistic designs. Unfortunately, this evergreen is not very hardy and is generally restricted to container growing in northern gardens. Baltic Ivy is a cold-hardy English type, grows 40 to 50 feet long, and is covered with similar, smaller leaves.

Boston Ivy is more closely related to another attractive vine, Virginia Creeper, than to true ivies. Boston ivy is deciduous. Its three-lobed, 4½-inch-wide leaves cover vines 60 feet long. Its native American cousin, Virginia Creeper, has a distinctive five-lobed leaf that turns to flaming red in the autumn. Another close relative, Lowes Ivy, is a slow growing vine that can be confined to low walls without losing its form.

Kenilworth Ivy is another ivylike vine that trails to a modest height of 5 feet. Small, rounded leaves are divided by 5 to 7 lobes. In warm climates, it may grow as a perennial, but northern gardeners generally treat it as an annual.

SITE & SOIL REQUIREMENTS

English Ivy will thrive in sun or shade as long as it has humus-rich, well-drained, moist soil. Winter sun in the northern parts of its range can cause leaves to drop; it should be protected from direct, winter sunlight. Boston Ivy and its close relatives fare equally well in sun or shade and are not especially fussy about soil types, except for Lowes Ivy, a type that craves the same good soil as the English varieties. Boston-type ivies do well in urban settings and are dependable near the seaside. Kenilworth Ivy prefers partial shade and will only thrive when it is kept in evenly moist, humus-rich soil. It thrives in greenhouses and is a wonderful container plant.

PLANTING

Ivies tend to take root quickly, and many grow at extraordinary rates. Plant the vines deeper than they were growing previously to encourage extra rooting. To plant rooted cuttings, set the vine in the ground well over the level of the last root. Prune back the tops to enable the roots to become established before having to support lavish top growth. New plants can easily be started by cutting off a piece of vine and by putting it in water; change the water frequently. Rooting powders and special starting media are available, but are rarely necessary for ivy.

TRELLISING

Ivy climbs by rootlike holdfasts that dig in and do not let go. The good news is that they can climb nearly any surface. The bad news is that they can damage wood, stone, concrete, or stucco. While a trellis is not necessary, it allows the vines to be trained to any imaginable design without sacrificing the primary structure. A trellis of wood lattice or 1x2 lumber is functional and versatile enough to fit many situations (see illustration on page 22).

GROWING TIPS

The rapid growth rate of English and Boston Ivies demands annual attention to pruning, or the support will be obliterated by rambling greenery. Some early pinching and snipping will add considerably to the general appearance of both varieties. Decide how you want them to look when they are fully grown, and prune them accordingly. Little feeding is necessary. A scoop of compost each spring is sufficient, and consistent watering is essential.

PESTS & DISEASES

Most ivies are remarkably pest free, although Japanese beetles occasionally attack Boston Ivy and its relatives. Aphids feed on English varieties, and many ivies may harbor spider mites.

Bacterial and fungal leaf spot sometimes occurs in ivies. Improve ventilation by thinning heavily matted vines, and cut out and destroy any diseased parts.

HONEYSUCKLE

Some northern gardeners think of honeysuckle as only a southern gardener's dream, while southerners may well consider these vines as rampant runaways. The truth is that there are honeysuckles that are hardy enough to thrive as far north as southern Canada and are modest enough in growth to grace even a tiny garden with their heady fragrance.

VARIETIES

Varieties of honeysuckles vary mostly in growth habit. Hall's Honeysuckle originated in Japan and took over much of the Mid-Atlantic with its overexuberant growth. This hardy, exceptionally fragrant vine makes some gardeners shudder at the thought of cultivating honeysuckle deliberately. The intricate scarlet blossoms of Trumpet Honeysuckle with its broad, semievergreen foliage make a beautiful display. The scentless, twining vines can reach up to 50 feet long, but do not overrun the garden like Hall's Honeysuckle.

Everblooming Honeysuckle is not as cold hardy as either of the other two varieties. The growth is much more compact with well-mannered vines that approach only about 10 feet in length. It is their lovely, deeply scented, rose-colored blossoms that steal your heart. Henry Honeysuckle flowers are not as showy as other varieties, but the dark green leaves and twining 15-foot stems form an attractive screen. It also produces bluish black berries that provide interest through much of the winter.

SITE & SOIL REQUIREMENTS

Most honeysuckles will do well either in sun or shade, except Everblooming which prefers full sun. Light or heavy soils are suitable for most, but Henry Honeysuckle prefers a rich loam with both good drainage and moisture retention. Other varieties are tolerant of drought and windy conditions.

PLANTING
Honeysuckles are easy to plant, and most grow quickly. Plant in the spring through early summer, as with other bare-root plants (see Blackberries, page 39), about 2 to 3 feet apart, and keep well watered.

When setting out a Hall's, take care not to place it too close to other plants or to full grown trees because the vigorous growth may engulf and smother any vegetative competition.

TRELLISING
Honeysuckles climb via their twining stems. They require a trellis, but will claim anything that they can wrap around. Plan on a grand scale for Hall's and Trumpet. Allow enough space, and build a sturdy trellis. Simple redwood or pine wooden fans or ladders are commonly used. Everblooming and Henry will fit nicely on a small corner trellis where two fences meet, or you could provide a small tepee or fan trellis. (See illustrations in Chapter 3 for ideas.) Honeysuckles can also be used as flowing ground covers.

GROWING TIPS
When grown in regions that are appropriate to the hardiness of their variety, honeysuckles are easy to cultivate. The only special attention that they require is spring pruning to keep their rambunctious growth under control. The limited growth of Everblooming requires less attention to pruning than other varieties; a quick snip or two after the vines finish flowering is all that is needed.

PESTS & DISEASES
Aphids will sometimes bother honeysuckle, especially the Trumpet variety. Seriously infested plants roll up their leaves with the pests inside and make pest control difficult. Otherwise, honeysuckles are such vigorous plants that pest or disease problems are rare.

MORNING GLORY

What picturesque country road would be complete without the random webs of morning glories that are draped over split rail fences or crooked mailboxes? These quick growing, climbing vines are definitely a part of rural Americana.

VARIETIES

While there are a few different colors from which to choose, all morning glories are similar. They are annuals and often grow to 10 feet high or more in a single season. The long vines are covered with heart shaped leaves and an abundance of large, funnel-like flowers that open in the morning and close by noon. Heavenly Blue is one of the most familiar varieties. Its white-throated, deep blue, blossoming vines climb to 8 feet high. The crimson-flowered Scarlet O'Hara reseeds for repeat performances. Scarlet Star produces rosy red flowers that are marked with a contrasting white star. Pearly Gates boasts pure white blossoms up to 4½ inches across. For shorter vines, Early Call is available in a range of colors on 3- to 6-foot-long vines. Another bright red variety, Cheerio, stays open during the day.

SITE & SOIL REQUIREMENTS

Morning glories prefer a sunny location. They prosper in fairly poor soil, and too fertile soil results in lots of vine and foliage at the expense of blossoms. A neutral to slightly alkaline pH level (7 to 8) suits them, and good drainage is a must.

PLANTING

Morning glories can be sown directly, but may be obstinate about germinating. Plant only after the soil is well warmed, and frost is long forgotten. To speed the process, notch the seeds with a small, sharp knife, or soak the seeds overnight in warm water. Morning glories dislike having their roots disturbed, so transplanting calls for care. Whether starting your own plants or putting in nursery plants, choose peat pots. At transplant time, set the seedlings in the pots in the ground, about 3 to 4 inches apart, and completely cover (see page 44).

TRELLISING

Morning glories are twining vines that will wrap themselves around any stationary object. A fence, trellis, arbor, or lamp post all cheerfully will be entangled. The vines are not heavy, so the strength of the support is not of prime concern. They can climb equally well on wood, wire, or twine. (See illustrations in Chapter 3 for ideas.)

GROWING TIPS

These vines are hard to discourage. They are closely related to bind-weed and have the same enthusiasm and stamina. They require no special care and ask for water only when drought threatens.

PESTS & DISEASES

Pests are uncommon on morning glories, but there are two insects that may visit the vines. The morning glory leaf cutter and the morning glory leaf miner will do what they can to spoil the foliage; keep fallen leaves cleaned up to interrupt their life cycles.

ROSE

The undisputed Queen of Flowers, the lovely, fragrant rose, was so dubbed over 2,500 years ago by the Greek poet, Sappho. That was long before the exquisite specimens that are so familiar to us were developed. Still, the rose had then, as it always will have, an undeniable allure; nothing says romance more than roses. Thus, the classic, trellised flower has come to be the climbing rose. (If you would like to share your love of roses with others, you might consider joining a rose association (see Appendix II).)

VARIETIES

Roses offer a diversity of color and scent that is second to none. A garden gate that is framed by an archway and draped with lavish, richly scented roses is an image not soon to be forgotten.

The term "climbing rose" encompasses a range of different growth and flowering types. The common denominator is that they all produce flexible stems that grow from about 10 to 30 feet long with flowers that form all along their length.

There are *climbing versions* of hybrid tea, grandiflora, floribunda, and polyantha roses; these are mutations of the bush roses of the same type. Pillar roses grow to only about 10 feet high and traditionally are trained upright. Old-time Rambler roses are the hardiest of the climbers. They burst out in clusters of small flowers in late spring. Wild or pasture roses are not only good climbers, but also are hardy and usually quite vigorous.

Blaze is a common, large-flowered variety that produces clusters of bright scarlet flowers throughout the spring and sporadically until frost. Chevy Chase is a medium red, hearty growing rambler. New Dawn is an excellent climber with silvery pink flowers and Golden Showers is an award-winning, yellow variety.

Climbing tea roses are the least cold hardy, but in suitably warm climates, their continuous flowering makes them extremely popular. High Noon is a golden yellow, climbing hybrid tea rose. In warm areas, it grows profusely; in cooler regions, it can be trained as a pillar rose. White flowering, climbing tea roses include Climbing Snowbird and the larger flowered White Dawn. Gloire De Dijon is a tender, pink-flowered, climbing tea rose that was introduced in 1853. It can still rival the newest varieties for vigorous growth and abundant blossoms.

SITE & SOIL REQUIREMENTS

Except for climates where the afternoon sun can roast the blooms on the vine, roses welcome full sun. In very hot areas, the protection offered by afternoon shade is very helpful. The regal rose prefers a slightly acid soil (pH 6.8). Although it graciously tolerates a range of soils, it simply cannot suffer wet roots. All roses demand excellent drainage.

PLANTING

Roses are big business. They are available nearly year-round, either as bare-root plants or in containers. Bare-root roses are sold in mail-order catalogues, from local nurseries, and in hardware stores and supermarkets in the late winter and early spring. This is the best time to buy. Not only are prices lower compared to potted roses, but also the selection is much better. Most importantly, bare-root roses that are planted in the early spring show the best vigor and have the best chance of success. They also inspire the winter weary gardener.

Bare-root roses are most often sold as two-year-old field grown plants. They are graded at harvest according to quality standards decided upon by the American Association of Nurserymen. A grade of number 1 is best. This means that prior to pruning for shipment, a climbing rose must have at least three healthy canes at least 24 inches long. To receive a grade of number 1½, the plant must have at least two good canes at least 18 inches long. Roses that are graded as number 2 stock need only two canes, at 12 inches long, and although they are sure to be cheaper, they are not always a bargain.

Even though it may mean sloshing through a cold, wet, late winter garden, be prepared to plant a new rose as soon as it arrives and while it is still dormant. Ideally this means preparing the soil bed months in advance so that it has time to mellow. If prepared in the fall for early spring planting, even fresh manure will have aged enough that it will not burn the roots. Otherwise, use only aged manures or compost in amending the planting soil. All your care and preparation for an early start may be rewarded in the very first year with showy, fragrant blossoms.

Plant roses like other bare-root plants (see Blackberries, page 39), but include an extra step. Rose roots are stiff and set in a circular pattern around the base of the plant. Once you have dug the planting hole, refill it part way with topsoil to form a cone that the roots can fit around. Make sure that there is no air space between the roots and the soil cone by carefully packing in the soil and watering to remove any air pockets. Using topsoil first, fill the hole completely until it is level with the ground. Then mound the soil over the base of the plant to the graft. Once new growth begins, carefully remove this soil. Spacing for roses varies greatly with varieties and the effect that you wish to create. Most require 3 to 4 feet between plants.

Container grown roses are also easy to plant, especially if the container is a fiber pot. These pots can go into the ground with the plant as long as they are first well watered and then well covered with soil (see page 44). Other containers, such as black plastic containers, must be carefully cut away. To plant, gently position the rose in the hole and refill with topsoil, then soil. Water deeply.

TRELLISING

Lacking the ability to twine, grasp, or dig in with rootlets, roses are not true climbers. They are leaners that weave in and out of the trellis to support themselves; often tying the stems to the trellis is necessary.

Roses can be trained to scramble over anything from fences to archways and arbors to gazebos and rooftops. (See illustrations in Chapter 3 for ideas.) Nature pushes them to grow straight up, but they produce more flowers when they are trained horizontally. Bending a cane downward slows its growth and forces many little side stems to sprout. These side stems form the most blossoms.

The first two or three years of a new climbing rose's life should be devoted entirely to achieving the desired size and shape. As the vines grow, tie them in place, about 1½ to 2 feet apart. Main stems will stiffen as the plant matures. For high walls or trellises, let the plant grow about 10 feet tall before training. When spreading the canes apart, bend them sideways from the base of the plant.

GROWING TIPS

Wild roses are a testament to the inherent hardiness of these flowers. Most roses today can survive under conditions of little water or nutrients, but to get a very impressive show of blossoms, you must treat them right. Climbers are among the least demanding of roses. Water them deeply to encourage deep roots; work in compost or other organic matter; protect from harsh weather; watch for pests and diseases.

To stay healthy and produce armloads of those romantic blossoms, roses must be pruned. Most pruning should be done in late winter to early spring, while the plant is still dormant or is just beginning to form flower buds. Remove dead or old canes and any canes that show obvious signs of sickness or injury. If removing an entire cane, cut it flush to the union bud (graft) to prevent any disease organisms from entering a stub. Make other cuts at a 45° angle, about ¼ inch above an eye, or bud.

Ramblers are best pruned after they finish flowering. Take out the spent canes and tie to the support any new, long canes that have formed from the base.

In many areas, winter protection is mandatory. Some roses are naturally hardy. Wild roses, shrub roses, and many old-fashioned roses will usually withstand temperatures as low as -10°F with no protection. Often they can freeze right to the ground with everything still coming up roses the next year. Many modern, climbing roses can be somewhat tender. Those that have hybrid tea ancestries are the most fragile with a lower temperature limit of about 10°F. The trailing stems are at risk of winter injury, and often not all growing tips mature before cold weather sets in.

Most cold damage is not due to the depth that the temperature plunges, but rather to changes, such as freezes and thaws. Moisture inside the canes

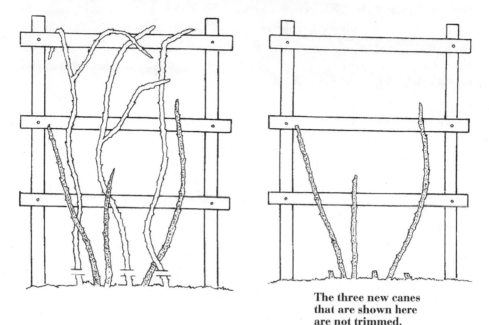

**The three new canes
that are shown here
are not trimmed.**

stresses cell walls by repeatedly expanding and shrinking as it turns to ice
then melts. Cold, dry winds threaten the plants with severe dehydration
because sleepy roots cannot draw up enough water from the soil to
compensate for the moisture loss. Warm winter lulls often fool the plants
into breaking dormancy, only to be hit by another round of freezing
temperatures.

Begin to steel your roses against the ravages of winter by withholding
any nitrogen based fertilizers at least 6 weeks prior to the first, expected
frost until the following spring. This helps to prevent tender, new growth.
Do not pluck late blossoms, but allow them to mature into rose hips. This
is nature's way of telling the plant that winter is coming, and the plant
reacts by ceasing growth and stockpiling solids within its cells. Solids
replace much of the moisture that is so vulnerable to freezing and thawing.

In very cold areas, roses should be covered for the winter. Perhaps
surprisingly, the object is not to bundle them up and keep them cozy and
warm, but to keep them cold, or more accurately, at a constant temperature. Climbers can be covered by untying the vines and laying them on the

ground or in a trench and by covering them with several inches of evergreen boughs, straw, or soil. The vines also may be left on the trellis and wrapped with burlap or old blankets that are stuffed with straw or other insulating material. Be sure to clean up any debris, dead leaves, or old canes before protecting your roses for the winter. Many diseases and pests hide undercover at ground level during the winter.

PESTS & DISEASES

The list of what ails the rose can be very discouraging. Mobs of sticky aphids clump around flower buds and other new growth. Thrips can ruin unopened blossoms with their sneaky, eating habits. Japanese beetles place roses high on their list of preferred foods. Borers devour inner stems and cause roses to suddenly droop. Several pests are so drawn to roses that they are named for them. For example, rose curculio, rose gall, rose leaf beetle, rose midge, and rose scale prefer roses almost exclusively. A big pest for rural gardeners is the supposedly timid deer. Roses trellised right to the side of the house are by no means off limits. Roses are especially at risk for deer in the winter when other forage is scarce.

Vintage roses are often much more resistant to disease than the newer varieties that are bred for beauty. Do consider disease resistance when you are selecting your climbers. Many diseases may target roses, but only a few threaten real damage. Black spot causes leaves to fall. Canker, which gains entry through injuries, such as those caused by frost damage, forms ulcerous sores. Powdery mildew coats the canes and the leaves with a white powder of fungal spores that feed on the surface of plant tissues; it weakens the plant and gives it an ungainly appearance. Rust causes bright orange spots under the leaves. Immaculate conditions greatly reduce the presence of infecting agents, and a watchful eye will alert you to any developments that may need treatment.

TRUMPET VINE

If you like the company of hummingbirds, plant a trumpet vine. These tropical looking vines are actually native to the southeastern United States. They grow up to 35 feet long and produce clusters of orange-red, trumpet shaped flowers at the tips. These showy blossoms draw the attention of nectar-sipping hummingbirds.

VARIETIES

The most widely available varieties are *Campsis radicans*, but other varieties can be found in some nurseries and specialty plant catalogues. Madame Galen is a cross between *C. radicans* and *C. grandiflora* and produces more dramatic flowers than either parent. All varieties blossom from July through September.

SITE & SOIL REQUIREMENTS

A trumpet vine asks only for a sunny spot and well-drained soil. It will grow well in either light or heavy soil and is a welcome ornamental in difficult, seaside areas.

PLANTING

Trumpet vines are most often sold as bare-root plants and should be planted accordingly (see Blackberries, page 39). Set the plants about 3 feet apart. They are fairly hardy and can become well established in their first year. They transplant well and climb and bloom in no time.

TRELLISING

Due to their exceptional growth, trumpet vines need a solid support. They climb by twining their stems and by using rootlike holdfasts. They will conquer stone, brick, or wooden walls, but the holdfasts can be damaging, especially to wooden surfaces. Trumpet vines can be trained along wooden or wire trellises. (See illustrations in Chapter 3 for ideas.) Despite their eager climbing habits, they often need periodic tying to hold up their weighty vines.

GROWING TIPS

Trumpet vines are easy to grow—almost too easy. They can quickly become a thick, tangled mass if not kept trimmed. Pruning should be done whenever necessary to prevent the stems from forming an interlocking, air strangling, stem stressing, unsightly heap. First snip out any dead or sick vines, and then remove those vines that grow into the plant mass. This encourages healthy, outward growth.

PESTS & DISEASES

The trumpet vine is rarely troubled by insects and usually disease free.

WISTERIA

Wisteria can bide its time, stubbornly refuse to bloom for years, or overflow with volumes of cascading blossoms. Old-fashioned, exotic, and exquisitely dramatic, a full blooming wisteria can turn any support into a stage.

VARIETIES

Wisteria varieties come in shades of lilac, pink, pink and white, and purple. The flowers dangle in grapelike clusters, often so thickly that they obscure their supports. Although there are native American species, Oriental imports are the most commonly grown.

Chinese wisteria, classified as *Wisteria sinensis* and Japanese wisteria, *W. floribunda,* are the most widely available. Chinese wisteria produces masses of violet-blue flowers in a stunning spectacle as all the flower buds explode into bloom at the same time. The lilac-colored flowers of Japanese wisteria characteristically unfold from the base of the cluster to the tip to reach an overall length of 18 inches or more. The Japanese blossoms are strongly perfumed. In southern states, this variety grows so enthusiastically, it can become a nuisance. Japanese wisteria is also the variety most likely to bloom in cooler climates. The trailing stems easily grow to 20 feet long and can exceed 40 feet if allowed. The intertwining trunks of this vine mature into wood up to 10 inches thick.

SITE & SOIL REQUIREMENTS

This plant must have its place in the sun. Anything less than full sun retards flowering. Never place a wisteria on the north side of a wall or building or in a position where it will be shaded. They also do not belong underneath overhangs or eaves or near living trees. Overhangs will shadow the vines and prevent rain from reaching the roots. While a sturdy tree may seem like the perfect support for the twining stems, the stems may soon choke the life from the tree. Japanese wisteria is a good choice for a seaside garden. It tolerates the salt air well and thrives in sandy, infertile soil.

All wisteria need well-drained soil that has been loosened at least 2 feet down; this gives the energetic roots room to sprawl. Soil high in nitrogen will promote much vegetation, but preclude flower formation. Although the vines will flourish, they are disappointing without that cascading wave of color. A weak soil, possibly amended with phosphorus, is preferable.

PLANTING

Wisteria are usually sold as grafted bare-root plants and graded according to quality. Select only a plant graded number 1.

Plant in late winter to early spring, while the plants are still dormant. Begin by preparing the soil to a depth of at least 2 feet. Loosen it well, and add sand or organic matter to lighten the texture and to improve the drainage. If planting more than one vine, space them 5 feet apart. Dig each hole deep enough to fashion a mound of topsoil in the hole. Arrange the roots around the mound. Trim any broken or very long roots from the plant, and position the plant so that the graft is above the soil line. Alternatively fill the hole with topsoil and water until level with the ground. Keep the new plants well watered until new growth begins.

TRELLISING

Wisteria is not one for an understated display. It is a glamorous beauty with theatrical aspirations. High and mighty aptly describe its requirements for supports. It demands a grand stage not only for growth, but also for visual balance. Wisteria looks cramped and out of placed when it is squeezed into a small space.

The massive vines have traditionally been trained up porch pillars and along horizontal beams so that the pendulous flowers flow over the edges. Stone or brick walls make an appropriate backdrop in terms of grand design and necessary strength. If a wooden structure is to serve as a support, it must be of high quality, heavy-duty lumber (see illustration on page 28).

The treelike vines climb by spiraling around their supports and each other. The trunks can be manually twisted or braided to add yet more interest; their rapid growth and natural twining tendencies make such training easy. Position the vines in place, stake, and tie with soft cord.

GROWING TIPS

Wisteria grows quickly and can live for decades. It will survive almost anywhere, but getting it to flower is never a sure thing. A dose of rock phosphate or other phosphorous-rich food that is gently worked into the soil around the base of the trunk during the late spring or early summer should inspire flower buds to form.

Keeping the ranging vines under control helps to divert some of the plant's energy into flowering. Root pruning is often recommended to slow the growth. With a sharpened shovel blade, cut into the soil around the trunk. Stay at least 2 feet away from the trunk to form a circle 4 to 6 feet across. The vines should also be pruned back by cutting 2 feet or more from the tips. Once the vines are established, regular mid-July and mid-August pruning will boost flowering as well as keep the vines orderly. Suckers may form at the base of the plant and should be removed.

Wisteria is notorious for its dubious commitment to flowering. Vines have been coddled for years only to frustrate the best efforts of their caregivers. Perhaps the shade of a tree that grew nearby was at fault, or the soil was a tad too rich. More often than not, the cause of its recalcitrant blooming is never discovered.

Although wisteria is hardy to zone 5, and many have thrived in zone 4 gardens, to cultivate them in northern climates is not for the faint of heart. The flower buds are exceptionally tender, and if caught by a late spring frost, they will succumb and end any hopes for that year's bloom.

To see a full flowering wisteria that is enveloping an arbor, porch, or doorway in all of its purple splendor and fragrant glory is to be forever enchanted. To call such a vine your own is to be vindicated, proud, and very lucky.

PESTS & DISEASES

Here, at last, is the best news. For all of its persnickety peculiarities, wisteria is one of the most trouble-free plants with no significant pests or diseases.

OTHER FINE VINES

Common Name Latin Name	Type	Hardiness	Sun Exposure
Akebia Five-leaf akebia *Akebia quinata*	Perennial	-10°	Sun or part shade
Bittersweet *Celastrus scandens*	Perennial	-40°	Sun or shade
Climbing hydrangea *Hydrangea anomala petiolaris*	Perennial	-20°	Sun or part shade
Dutchman's-pipe *Aristolochia durior*	Perennial	-10°	Sun or shade
Hops *Humulus lupulus*	Perennial	-30°	Sun
Humulus japonicus	Annual		Sun
Moonflower Moonvine *Ipomoea alba*	Annual		Sun
Nasturtium *Tropaeolum majus*	Annual		Sun
Passionflower *Passiflora caerulea*	Perennial	5° to 10°	Sun
Scarlet runner bean *Phaseolus coccineus*	Annual (N) Perennial (S)	Tender	Sun
Silver lace vine Chinese fleece vine *Polygonum aubertii*	Perennial	-20°	Sun
Sweet pea *Lathyrus odoratus*	Annual		AM Sun PM Shade
Wintercreeper *Euonymus fortunei carrierei*	Perennial	-30°	Sun or shade

Method of Growth	Length of Growth	Description
Twines	30 to 40 feet	Vigorous. Prune fall or early spring. Use sturdy trellis.
Twines	35 feet	Showy, orange fruit clusters in fall. Needs large trellis.
Clinging holdfasts		Showy, snowy flowers. Prune winter or early spring.
Twines	30 feet	Often starts slowly, then suddenly grows. Needs sturdy trellis.
Twines	25 feet	Susceptible to insects. Fruits used to flavor beer.
Twines	25 feet	
Twining stems	30 feet	Pure white flowers open at dusk in 1 minute or less.
Weaves	3 to 7 feet	Prefers fairly weak soil. Grows quickly with many fragrant flowers.
Tendrils	20 feet	Fantastic flowers. Needs strong trellis and drastic fall or spring pruning.
Tendrils with adhesive discs	30 to 40 feet	Vigorous, fast growing vines. Deep scarlet, trumpet shaped flowers.
Twines Leans	20 feet	Hardy, drought tolerant. Rapid growth.
Tendrils	5 to 8 feet	Large pea blossoms. Colorful and fragrant.
Rootlike holdfasts	40 feet	Good for stone or brick. Glossy foliage. Likes cool summers.

Appendix II

MAIL-ORDER SUPPLIERS & PRODUCTS

Your local nursery or garden center is likely to carry a variety of trellising products, plants, and seeds. To order by mail or to obtain product information, consult the companies listed below.

This is only a partial listing. *The Complete Guide to Gardening by Mail* is available from The Mailorder Association of Nurseries, Dept. SCI, 8683 Doves Fly Way, Laurel, MD 20723. Please add $1.00 for postage and handling.

SEEDS & PLANTS

W. Atlee Burpee & Co.
Warminster, PA 18974
(exotic melons)

Gurney Seed & Nursery Co.
110 Capital Street
Yankton, SD 57079

Henry Field's Seed & Nursery Co.
415 North Burnett
Shenandoah, IA 51602

Park Seed Co.
Cokesbury Road
Greenwood, SC 29647-0001
(Basella Malabar)

Kurt Bluemel, Inc.
2740 Greene Lane
Baldwin, MD 21013

Comstock, Ferre & Co.
263 Main Street
PO Box 125
Wethersfield, CT 06109

Harris Garden Trends Co.
60 Saginaw Drive
Rochester, NY 14623

Heritage Gardens
1 Meadow Ridge Road
Shenandoah, IA 51601
(flowering trees and vines)

Jackson & Perkins Co.
2518 S. Pacific Highway
PO Box 1028
Medford, OR 97501
(planting stock including roses, fruit, and vegetables)

Johnny's Selected Seeds
Albion, ME 04910

J.W. Jung Seed Co.
Box 340
335 S. High Street
Randolph, WI 53957

Kelly Nurseries
Catalog Division
Louisiana, MO 63353
(nursery stock including fruit and ornamental trees and vines)

Earl May Seed & Nursery
208 N. Elm Street
Shenandoah, IA 51603

Mellinger's, Inc.
2310 W. South Range Road
North Lima, OH 44452

J.E. Miller Nurseries
1524 W. Lake Road
Canandaigua, NY 14424

Nichols Garden Nursery
1190 N. Pacific Highway
Albany, OR 97321

R.H. Shumway
628 Cedar Street
PO Box 777
Rockford, IL 61105

Stokes Seeds, Inc.
737 Main Street
PO Box 548
Louisiana, MO 63353

Territorial Seed Co.
PO Box 27
80030 Territorial Road
Lorane, OR 97451
(vegetable seeds for the Pacific Northwest)

Thompson & Morgan
Dept. 13-0, PO Box 1308
Jackson, NJ 08527

Wayside Gardens
PO Box 1
1 Garden Lane
Hodges, SC 29695

White Flower Farm
Route 63
Litchfield, CT 06759

CANADIAN SOURCES:

Alberta Nurseries
PO Box 20
Bowden, AB T0M 0K0
(vegetables and flowers for short-season climates)

McConnell Nurseries
Port Burwell, ON N0J 1T0

Mc Fayden Seed Co.
30 Ninth Street
Box 1800
Brandon, MB R7A 6N4

Stokes Seeds
39 James Street
Box 10
St. Catharines, ON L2R 6R6

W.H. Perron
515 Labelle Blvd.
Chomeday Laval, QC H7V 2T3

FRUIT TREES, BERRIES & GRAPES
Stark Bro's Nurseries
Louisiana, MO 63353

A FRAME TRELLIS & NETTING
W. Atlee Burpee & Co.
Warminster, PA 18974

TRELLIS NETTING
Gurney Seed & Nursery Co.
Yankton, SD 57079

BEAN TOWERS
Henry Field's Seed & Nursery Co.
415 North Burnett
Shenandoah, IA 51602

TOMATO CAGES
Park Seed Co.
Cokesbury Road
Greenwood, SC 29647-0001

LEVER LOOP TRELLIS CLIPS
Gardener's Eden
PO Box 7307
San Francisco, CA 94120-7307

SOFT TRELLIS TIES
Gardener's Supply
128 Intervale Road
Burlington, VT 05401

TUTEURS
Gardener's Eden
PO Box 7307
San Francisco, CA 94120-7307

VERTICAL VEGGIES
Gardener's Supply
128 Intervale Road
Burlington, VT 05401

WALL O'WATERS
Gardener's Supply
128 Intervale Road
Burlington, VT 05401

TRELLEX
Kinsman Company, Inc.
River Road
Point Pleasant, PA 18950

BACILLUS THURINGIENSIS (BT)
Gardens Alive!
Hwy 48, PO Box 149
Sunman, IN 47041

PREDATOR SCENT
Bio-Pest Control Co.
401347FGS
New York, NY 11240

RED SPHERE TRAPS
Gardens Alive!
Hwy 48, PO Box 149
Sunman, IN 47041

BENEFICIAL INSECTS

Association of Applied Insect
Ecologists
100 N. Winchester Blvd.
Suite 260
Santa Cruz, CA 95050

Bio-Control Co.
PO Box 337
57A Zink Road
Berry Creek, CA 95916

Bio-Resources
PO Box 902
1210 Birch Street
Santa Paula, CA 93060

Natural Gardening Research
Center
Highway 48
PO Box 149
Sunman, IN 47041

Reuter Labs, Inc.
8540 Natural Way
Manassas Park, VA 22111

Rincon-Vitove Insectaries
PO Box 475
Rialto, CA 92376

Unique Insect Control
5504 Sperry Drive
Citrus Heights, CA 95621

NATURAL FERTILIZERS & SOIL AMENDMENTS

The Fertrell Co.
PO Box 265
Bainbridge, PA 17502

Francis Laboratories
1551 East Lafayette
Detroit, MI 48207

Green Earth Organics
9422 144th Street East
Puyallup, WA 98373

Mellinger's, Inc.
2310 W. South Range Road
Lima, OH 44452

Nitron Industries
4605 Johnson Road
PO Box 1447
Fayetteville, AR 72702

Ringer Corporation
9959 Valley View Road
Eden Prairie, MN 55344

Super Natural American
Distributing Co.
13906 Ventura Boulevard
Sherman Oaks, CA 91423

Zook & Ranck, Inc.
RD 2, Box 243
Gap, PA 17527

NATURAL GARDENING PRODUCTS

Dyna-Prep, Inc.
2215 Broadway
Yankton, SD 57078

Fairfax Biological Lab, Inc.
Clinton Corners, NY 12514

Green Pro Services
380 S. Franklin Street
Hempstead, NY 11550

Growing Naturally
PO Box 54
149 Pine Lane
Pinesville, PA 18946

Ohio Earth Food, Inc.
13737 Duquette Avenue NE
Hartville, OH 44632

Perma-Guard
1701 E. Elwood Street
Phoenix, AZ 85040

Safer, Inc.
60 William Street
Wellesley, MA 02181

OTHER PRODUCTS
Country Home Products
Ferry Road
PO Box 89
Charlotte, VT 05445
(pruners and various garden tools)

Garden Way, Inc.
102nd Street & 9th Avenue
Troy, NY 12179-0009
(garden tools)

Kemp Company
160 Koser Road
Lititz, PA 17543
(compost containers and tumblers)

Mantis Manufacturing Co.
1458 County Line Road
Huntingdon Valley, PA 19006
(garden equipment)

The Plow & Hearth
301 Madison Road
PO Box 830
Orange, VA 22960
(gardening tools and accessories)

Smith & Hawken
25 Corte Madera
Mill Valley, CA 94941
(gardening tools, planting stock, and gardening trellises)

ROSE ASSOCIATIONS
Contact local nurseries or parks for information on local rose societies or write:

The American Rose Society
PO Box 30,000
Shreveport, LA 71130
(Inquire about their Consulting Rosarian Program for advice on rose culture in your area.)

Canadian Rose Society
Mrs. B. Hunter
20 Portico Drive
Scarborough, ON M1G 3R3

Heritage Roses Group
Miriam Wilkins
925 Galvin Drive
El Cerrito, CA 94530
($5.00 subscription to The Rose Letter*)*

FURTHER READING

All About Growing Fruits, Berries & Nuts. San Francisco, CA: Chevron Chemical Company, 1987.

Cox, Jeff. *From Vines to Wines: The Complete Guide to Growing Grapes and Making Your Own Wine.* Pownal, VT: Garden Way Publishing, 1988.

Crockett, James Underwood. *Roses.* New York: Time-Life Books, 1971.

Editors of Garden Way Publishing. *Pruning Trees, Shrubs, and Vines (A-54).* Pownal, VT: Garden Way Publishing, 1980.

Editors of Garden Way Publishing. *Roses: 1001 Gardening Questions Answered.* Pownal, VT: Garden Way Publishing, 1989.

Hart, Rhonda Massingham. *Bugs, Slugs & Other Thugs: Controlling Garden Pests Organically.* Pownal, VT: Storey Publishing, 1991.

Hedrick, U.P. *Fruits for The Home Garden.* New York: Dover Publications, Inc., 1973.

Hill, Lewis. *Fruits & Berries for the Home Garden (Completely Revised & Updated Edition).* Pownal, VT: Garden Way Publishing, 1992.

Hill, Lewis. *Pruning Simplified.* Pownal, VT: Garden Way Publishing, 1986.

Hill, Lewis. *Secrets of Plant Propagation.* Pownal, VT: Garden Way Publishing, 1985.

Kramer, Jack. *Your Trellis Garden: How to Build It, How to Grow It, How to Show It.* New York: Walker and Company, 1976.

Lee, Hollis. *Orchard Handbook*. Barrington, IL: Countryside Books, AB Morse Company, 1978

McGill, Marion and Pye, Orrea. *The No-Nonsense Guide to Food & Nutrition*. Piscataway, NJ: New Century Publishers, Inc., 1981.

Osborne, Robert A. *Hardy Roses: An Organic Guide to Growing Frost- and Disease-Resistant Varieties*. Pownal, VT: Garden Way Publishing, 1991.

Oster, Maggie. *10 Steps to Beautiful Roses (A-110)*. Pownal, VT: Garden Way Publishing, 1989.

Perkins, Harold O. *Espaliers and Vines for The Home Gardener*. Ames, IA: The Iowa State University Press, 1979.

Proulx, Annie. *Great Grapes! (A-53)*. Pownal, VT: Garden Way Publishing, 1980.

Raymond, Dick. *Down-to-Earth Gardening Know-How for the 90s: Vegetables & Herbs*. Pownal, VT: Storey Publishing, 1991.

Riotte, Louise. *Berries, Rasp & Black (A-33)*. Pownal, VT: Garden Way Publishing, 1979.

Roses. Menlo Park, CA: Sunset Books, Lane Publishing Company, 1989.

Yepsen, Roger B. Jr. *The Encyclopedia of Natural Insect and Disease Control*. Emmaus, PA: Rodale Press, 1984.

INDEX

Page numbers in *italics* indicate illustrations.

trellising and, 5–6
Dutchman's-pipe, 140–141
Dwarf fruit trees, 97. *See also* specific trees

E

English Ivy, 124. *See also* Ivy
Erect blackberries, 38, 40. *See also*
    Blackberries
Espalier, 93–120
    defined, 93
    designs, 93–96, *95–96*
        apple trees, 105
        apricot trees, 114–115
        cherry trees, 111
        nectarine trees, 114–115
        peach trees, 114–115
        pear trees, 109
        plum trees, 118–119
    formal, 94–96
    frames for, 20
    planting trees for, 97–98
    trellises for, 30, 100
European plums, 117–118. *See also* Plum trees
Everbearing raspberries, 67–68. *See also*
    Raspberries

F

Fan espalier, 96, *96*
    training system, 50, *51*, 52, 103–104
Fasteners, 13–16
Fava beans, 34. *See also* Beans
Fences, 20–22, *22–23*
    espalier frames for, 30
    posts for, 10, *22*
    tomatoes, 88, *89*
    trellised plants and, 4
    wire mesh, 12–13
Fiberglass stakes, 11
Fiber pots, 44
Five-leaf akebia, 140–141
Floribunda rose, 129. *See also* Rose
Flower bud, 98, *98*
Flowering vines, 121–141
Formal espalier, 94–96
Framework for trellises, 9–11
Free-form fan, *96. See also* Fan espalier
Freestanding raspberries, 67. *See also*
    Raspberries
French prune, 117. *See also* Plum trees
Fruit. *See* Fruit trees; specific fruit trees
Fruit spur, 98, *98*
Fruit thinning
    apple trees, 106
    plum trees, 119
Fruit trees, 93–120

G

Galvanized pipe, 10
Galvanized steel fence posts, 10
Garden
    container, 16–18
    organic, 3
    shade in, 4
    space, trellising and, 3
Garden fabric, 4–5, 26
Gardening, organic, 3
Gourds, 72–79
Grandiflora rose, 129. *See also* Rose
Grapes, 12, 47–55
Greenhouses, mini, 4
Gridiron pattern, 94–96, *96*
    training system, 102
Growing tips
    apple trees, 105–106
    apricot trees, 115–116
    beans, 36–37
    blackberries, 40–41
    cherry trees, 111–112
    clematis, 123
    cucumbers, 45–46
    gourds, 75–76
    grapes, 53–54
    hardy kiwis, 58
    honeysuckle, 127
    ivy, 125–126
    malabar spinach, 33
    melons, 61–62
    morning glory, 129
    nectarine trees, 115–116
    peach trees, 115–116
    pear trees, 109
    peas, 66
    plum trees, 119
    raspberries, 71–72
    rose, 132–134
    squash, 75–76
    sweet potatoes, 81–82
    tomatoes, 90–91
    trumpet vine, 135
    wisteria, 137–138

H

Hardware for trellis, 16
Hardy kiwis, 55–58
Harvesting
    apples, 107
    apricots, 116–117
    beans, 37–38
    blackberries, 42
    cherries, 112–13